Fantastical Colorable Creatures

An Adult Coloring Book

by Richard McConochie

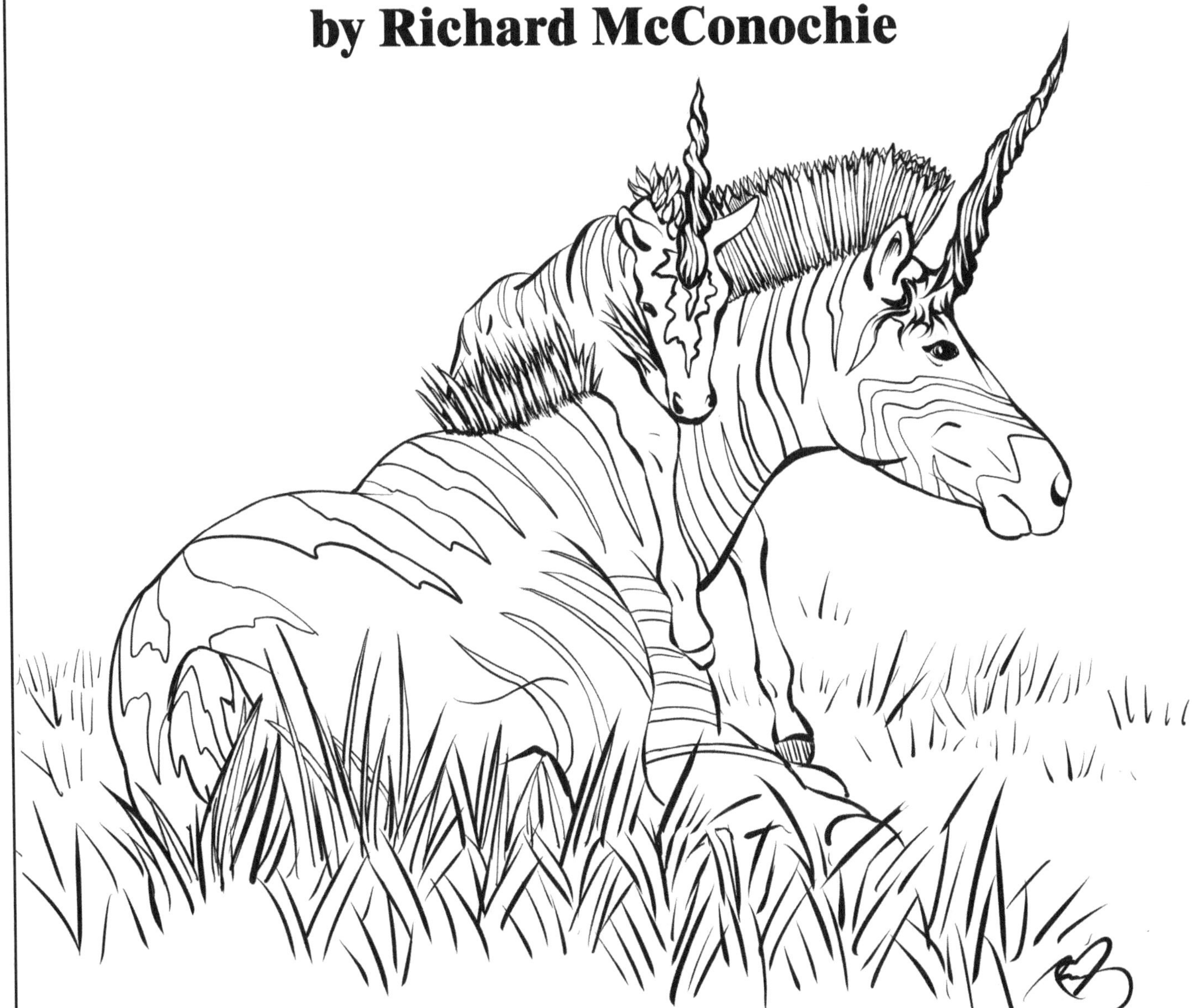

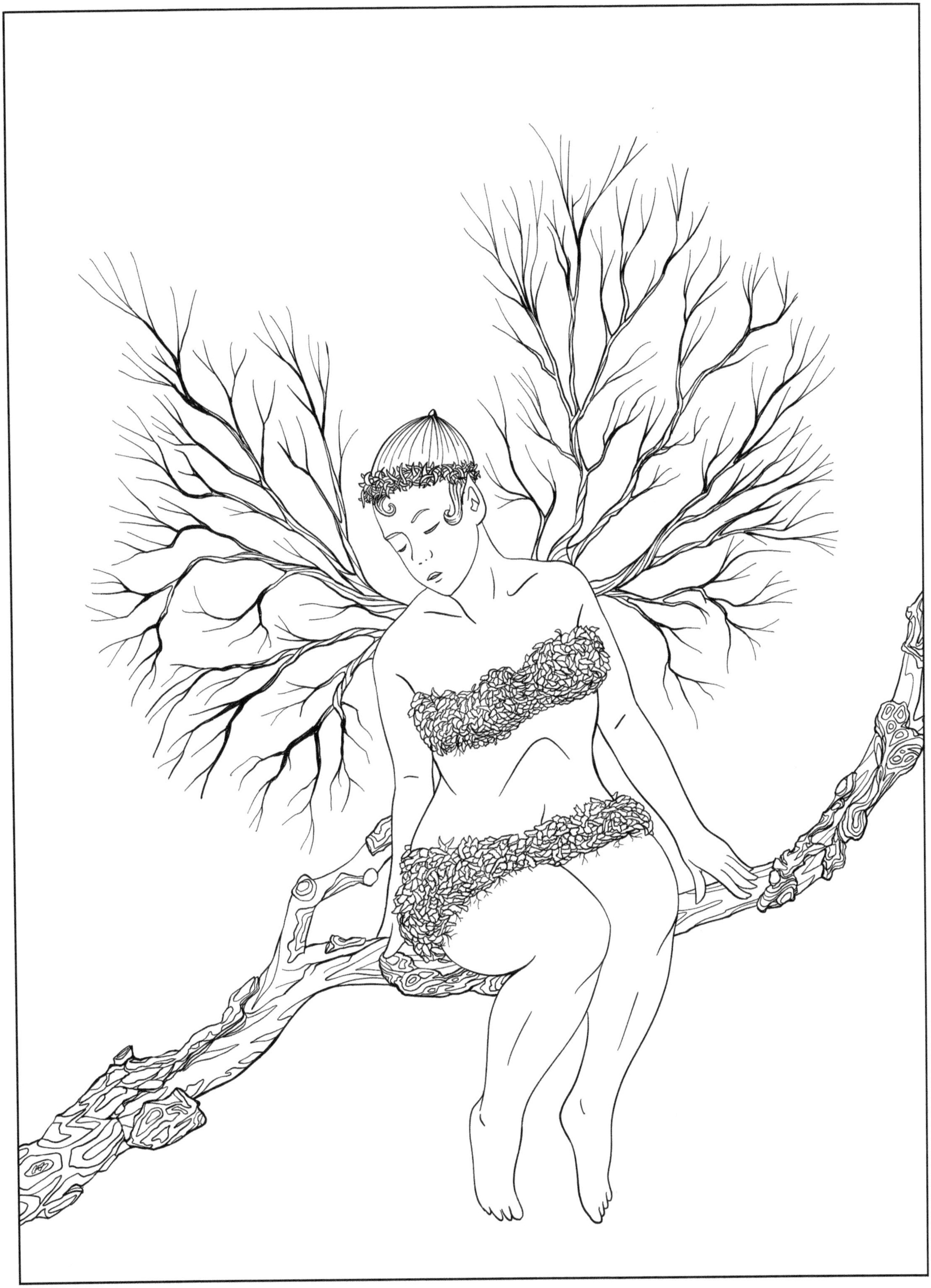

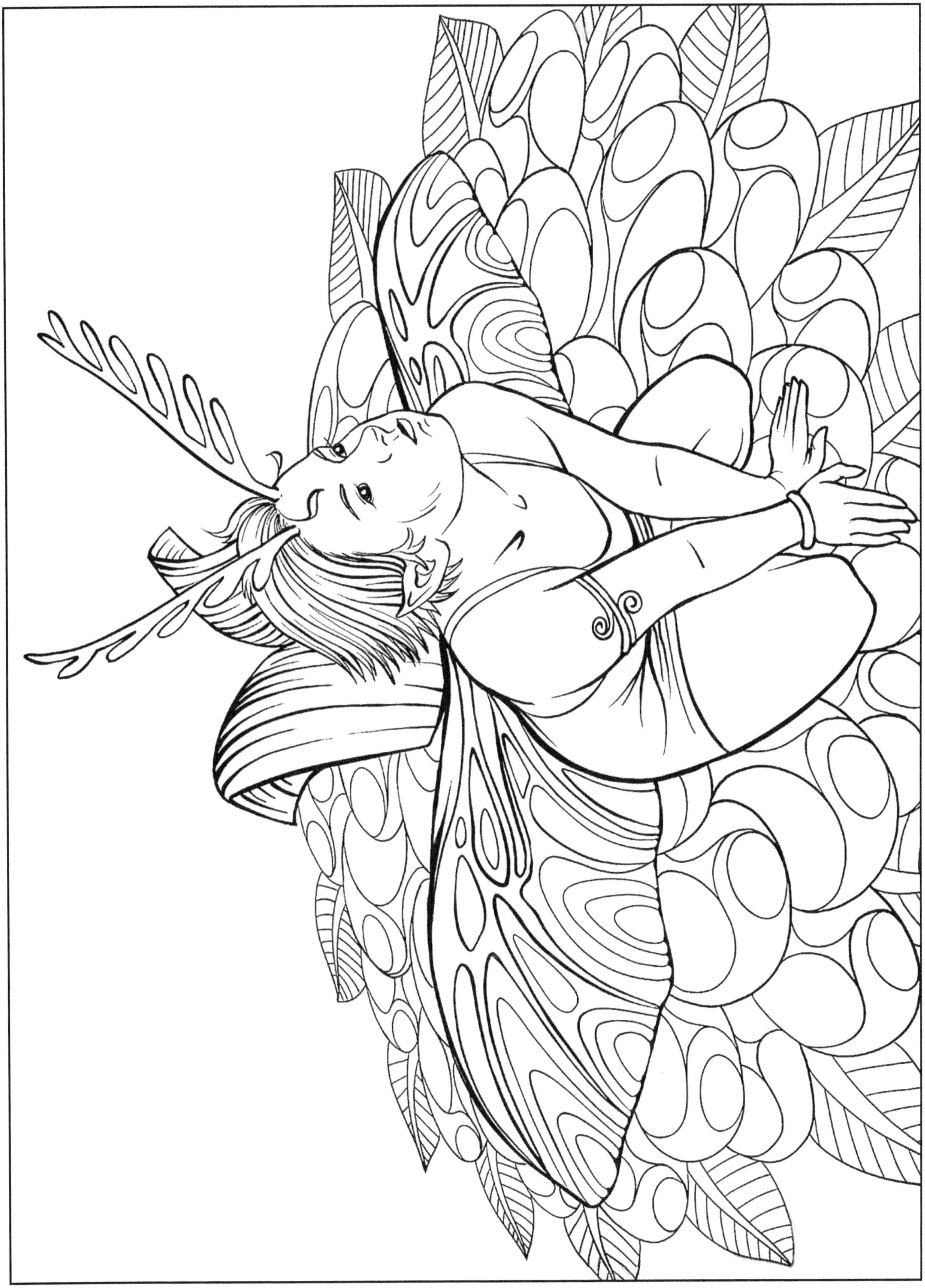

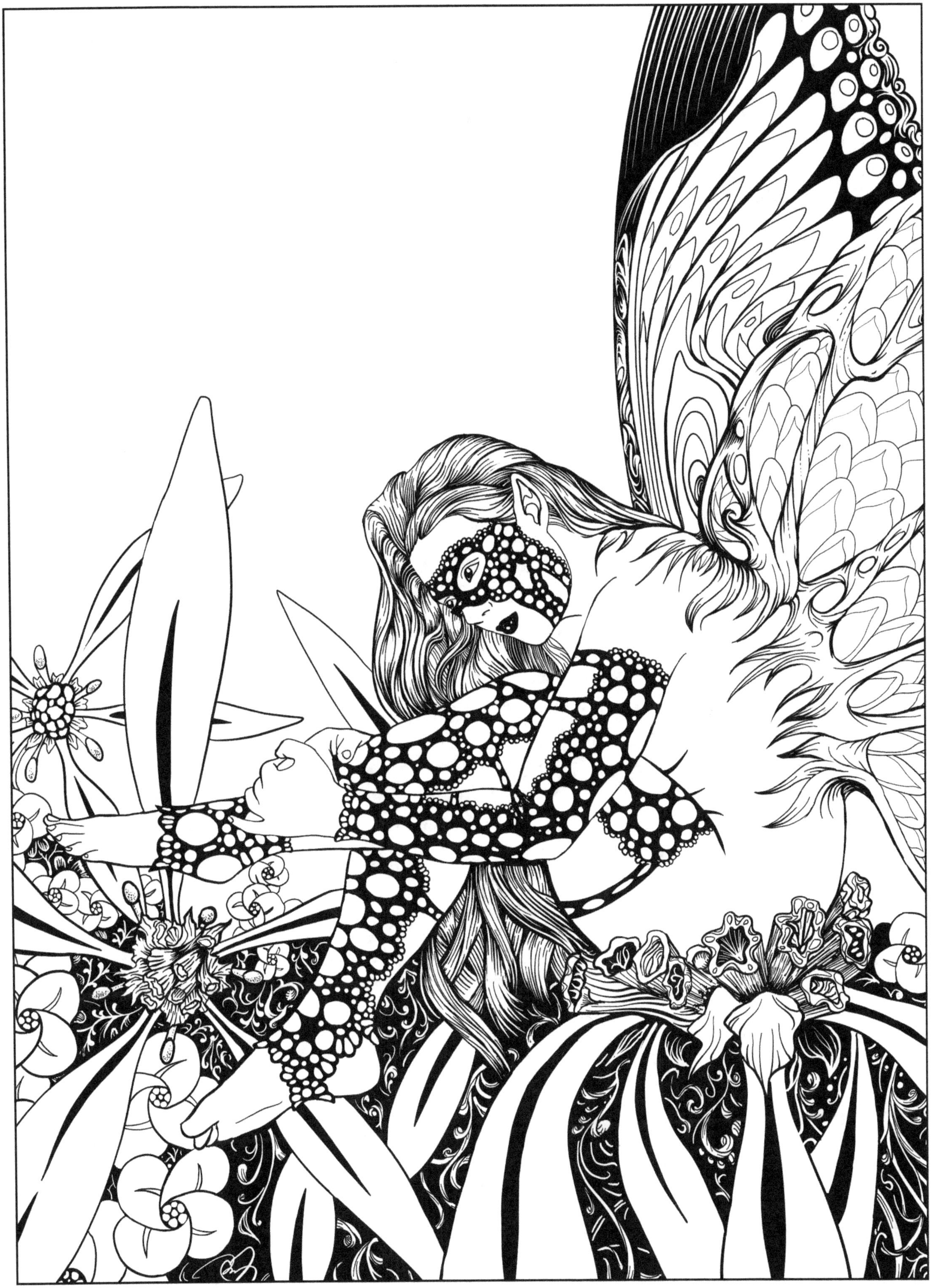

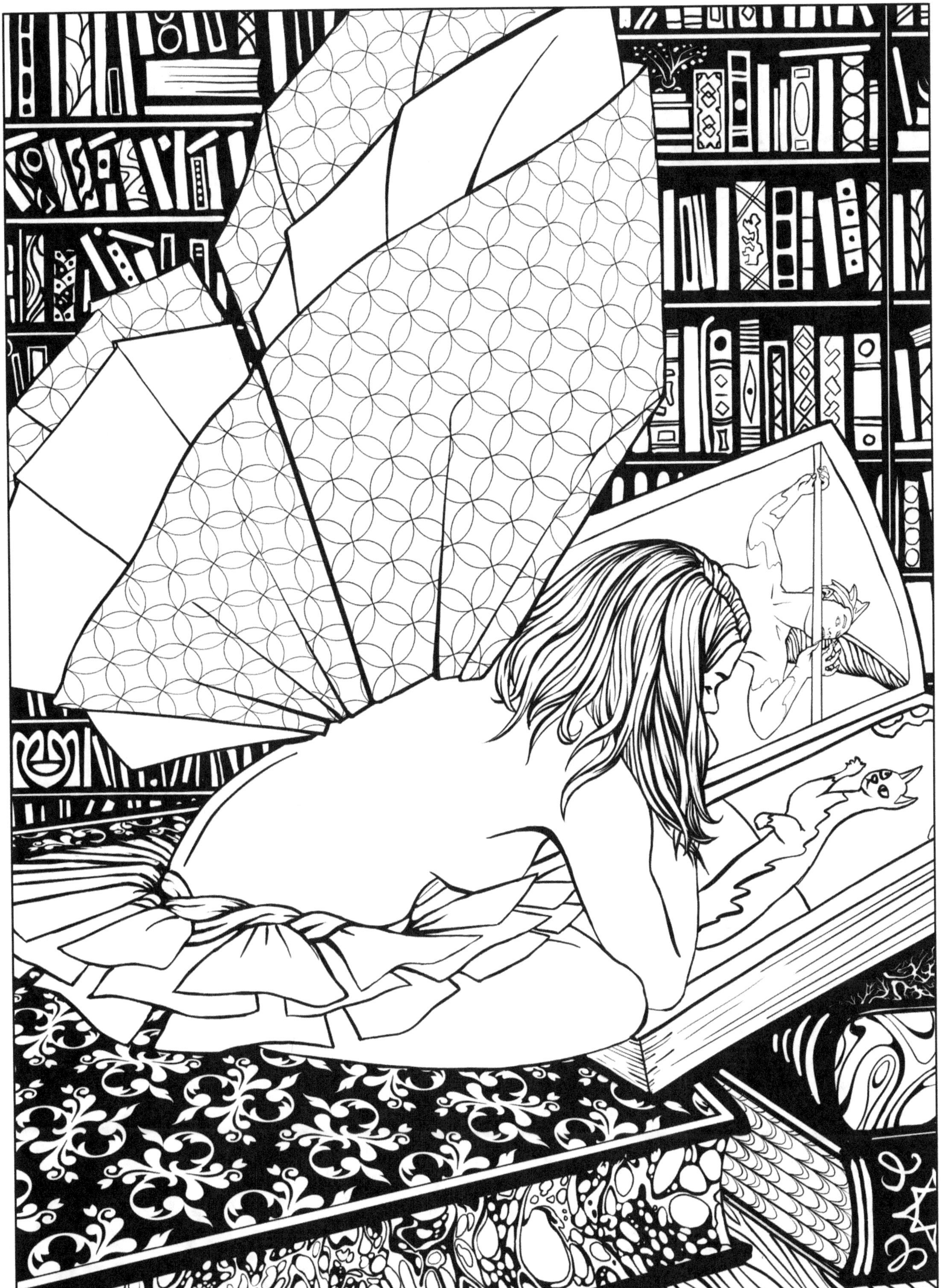

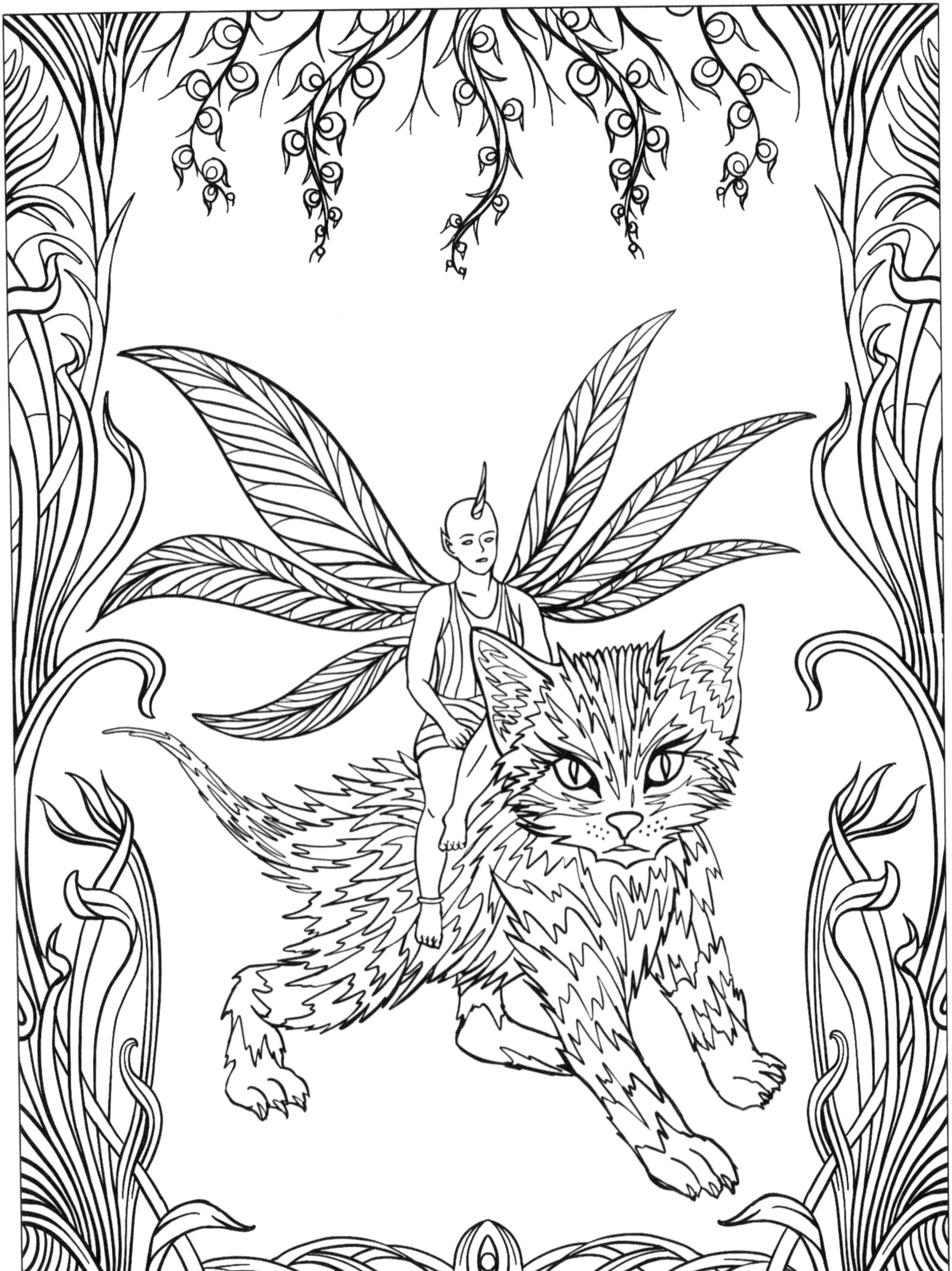

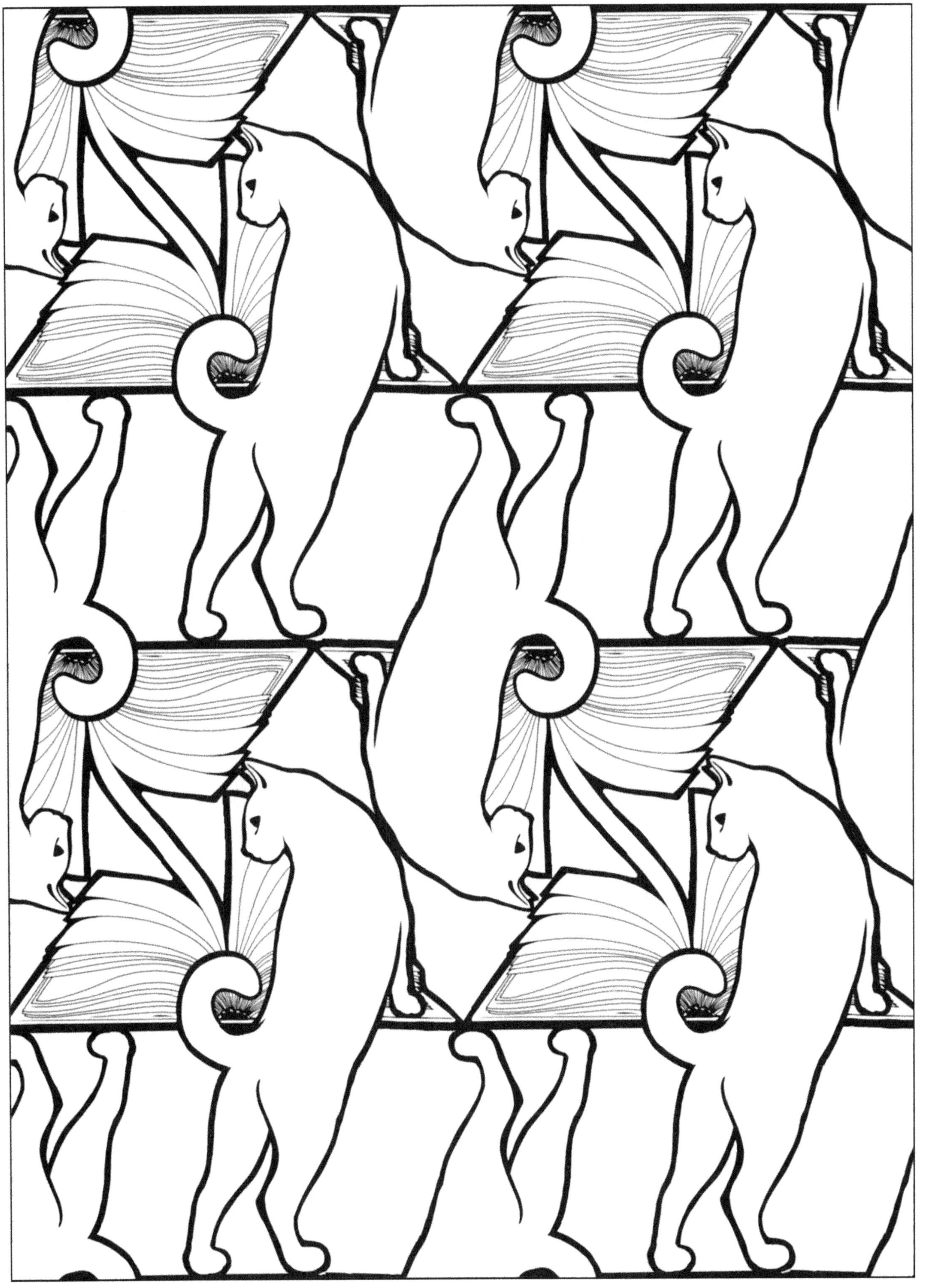

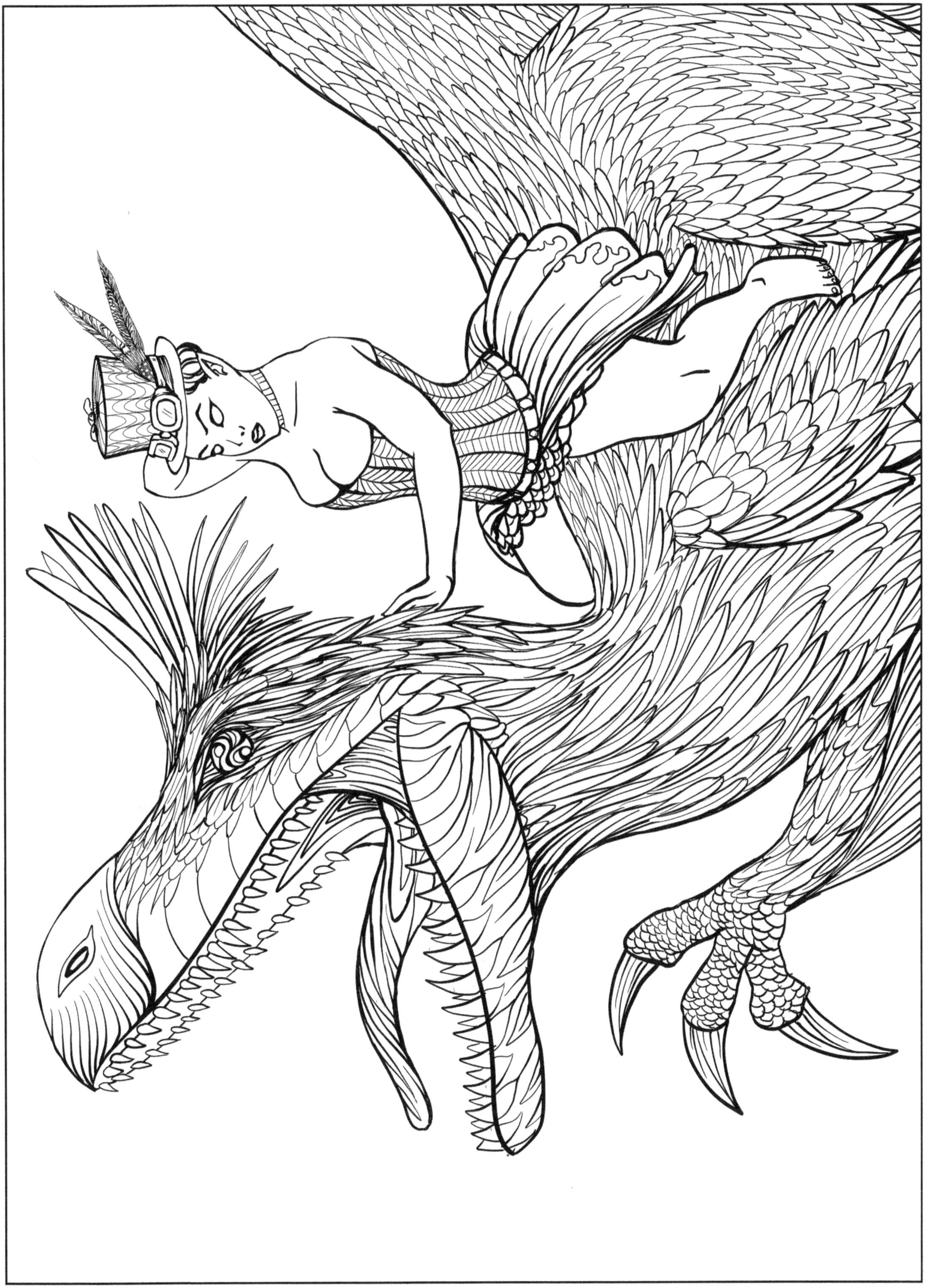

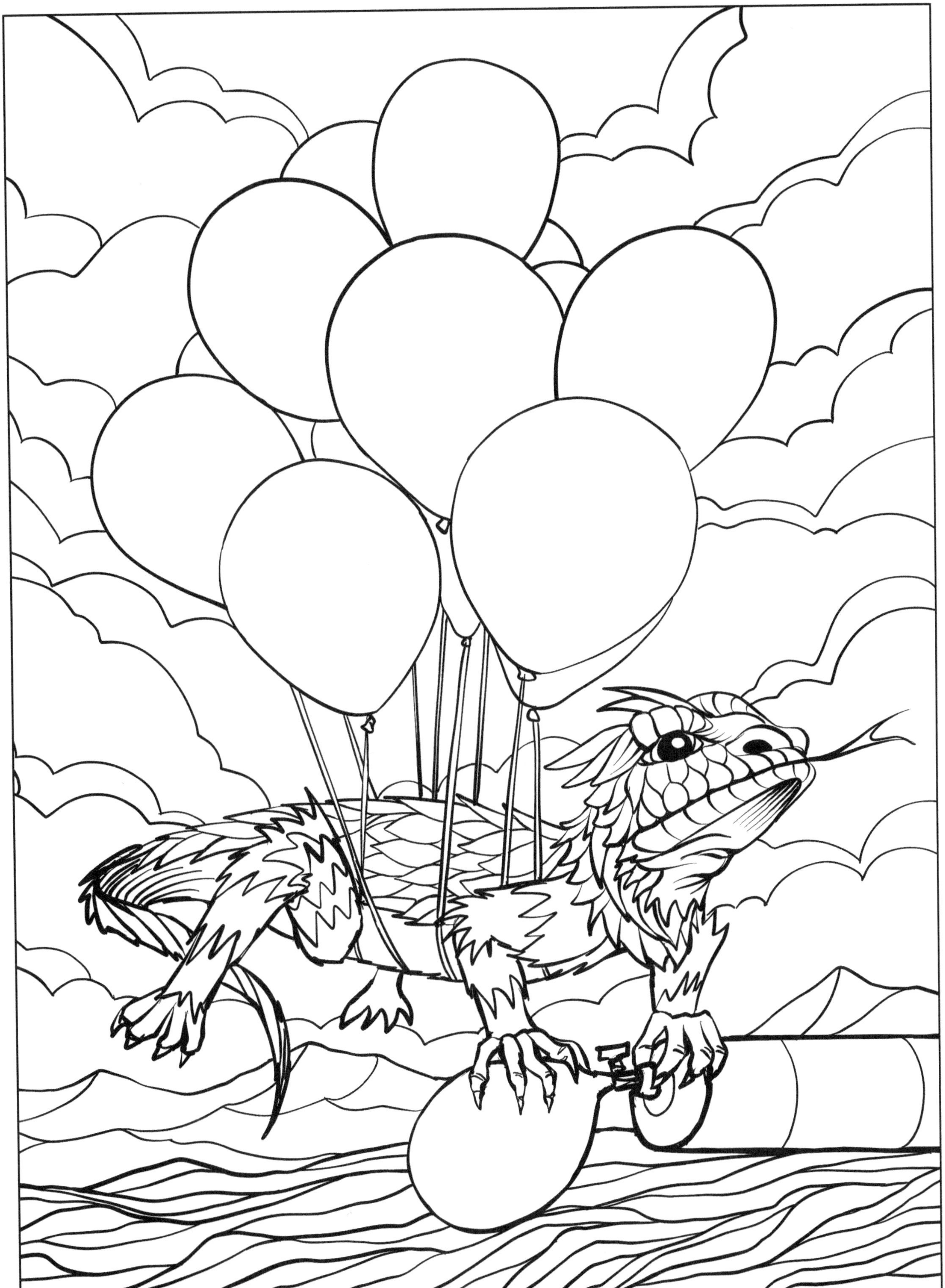

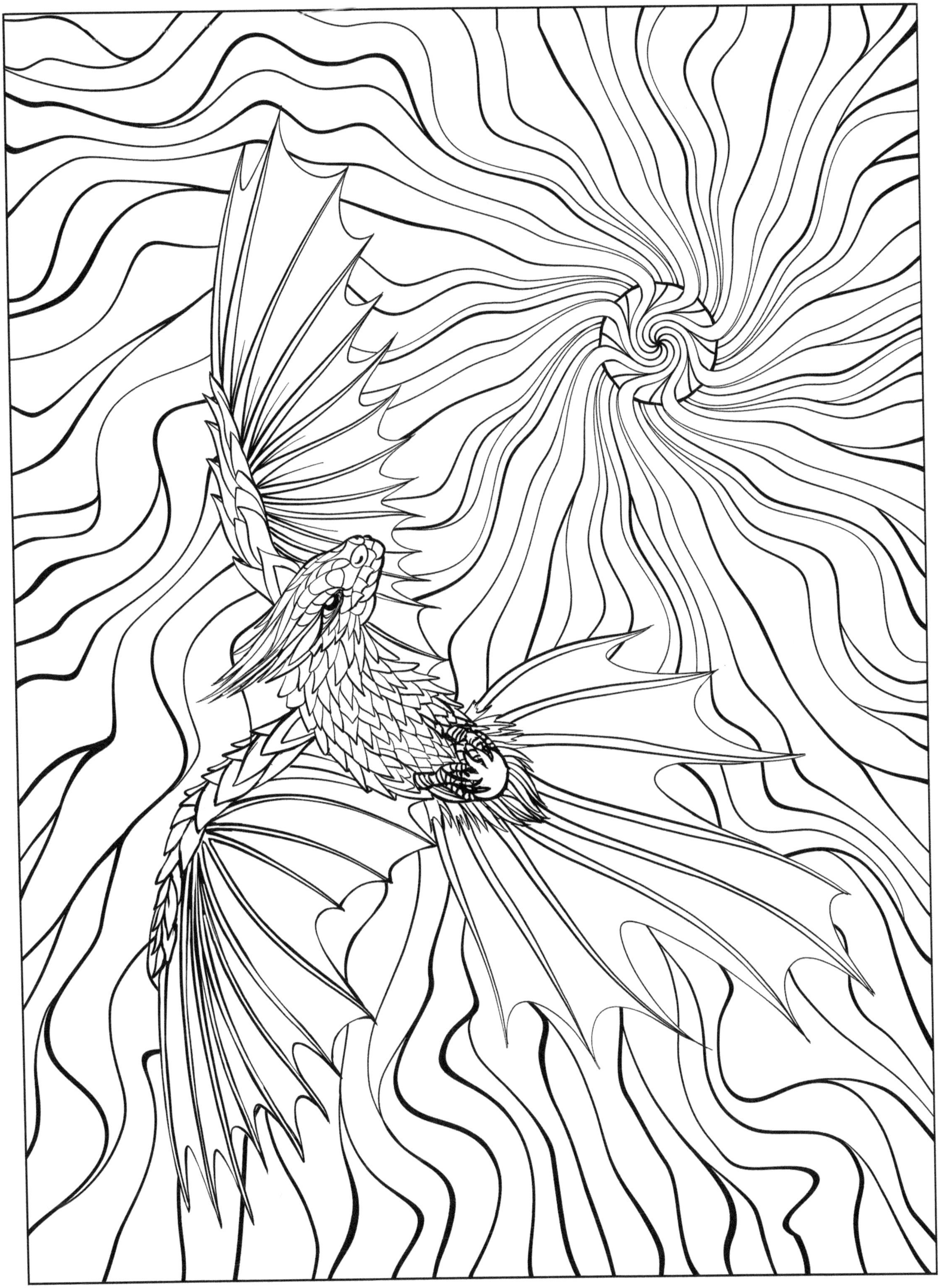

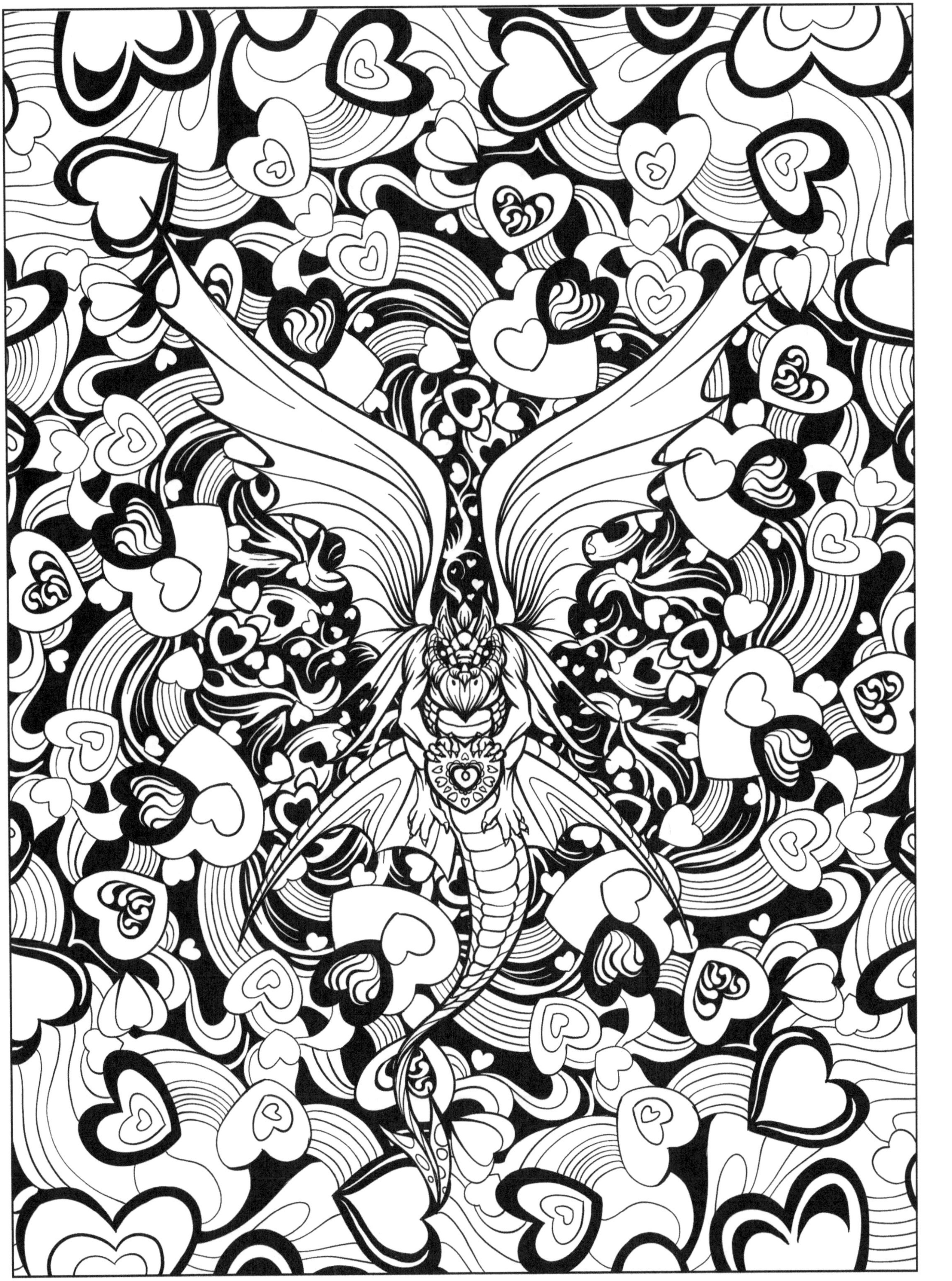

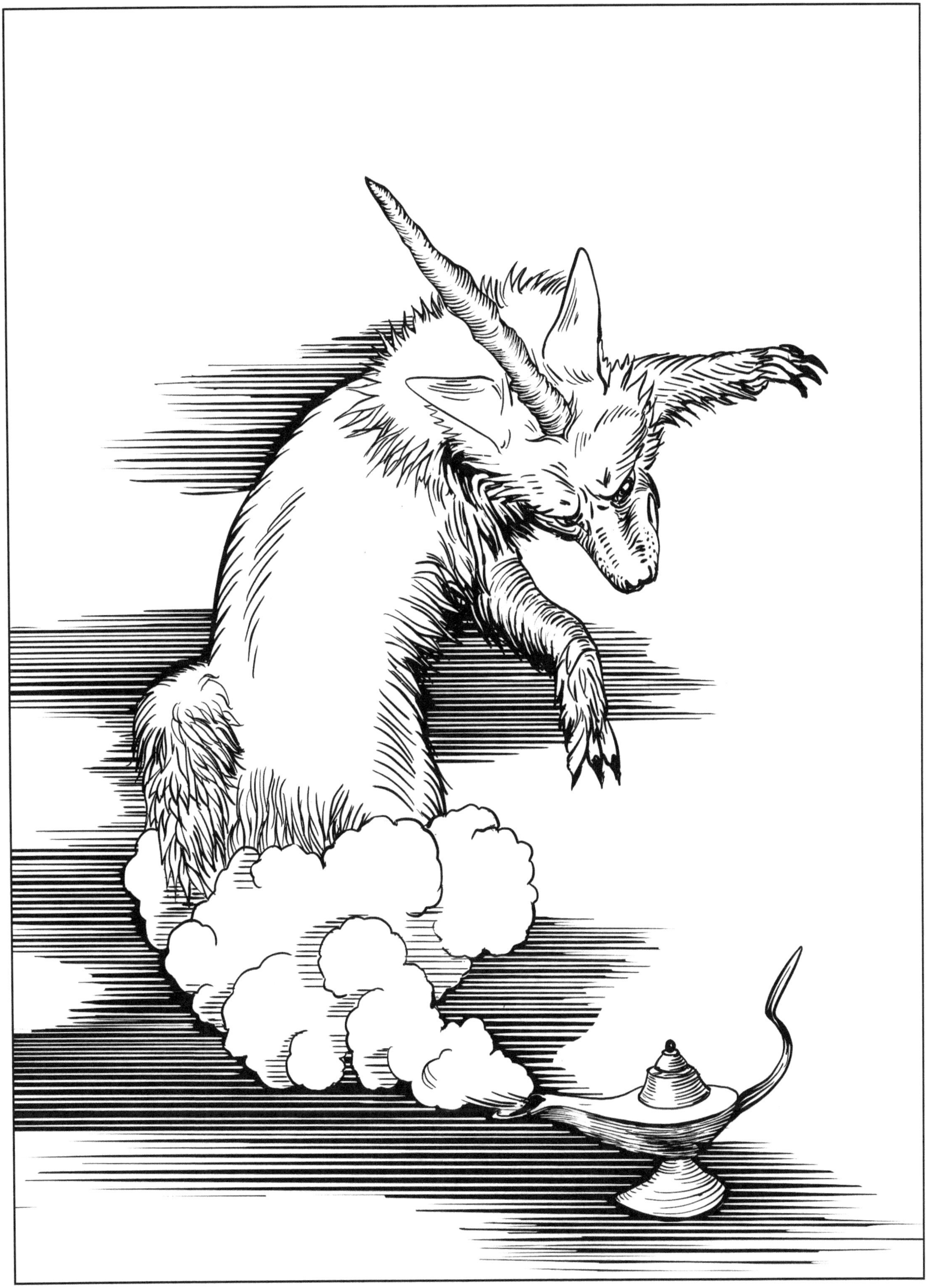

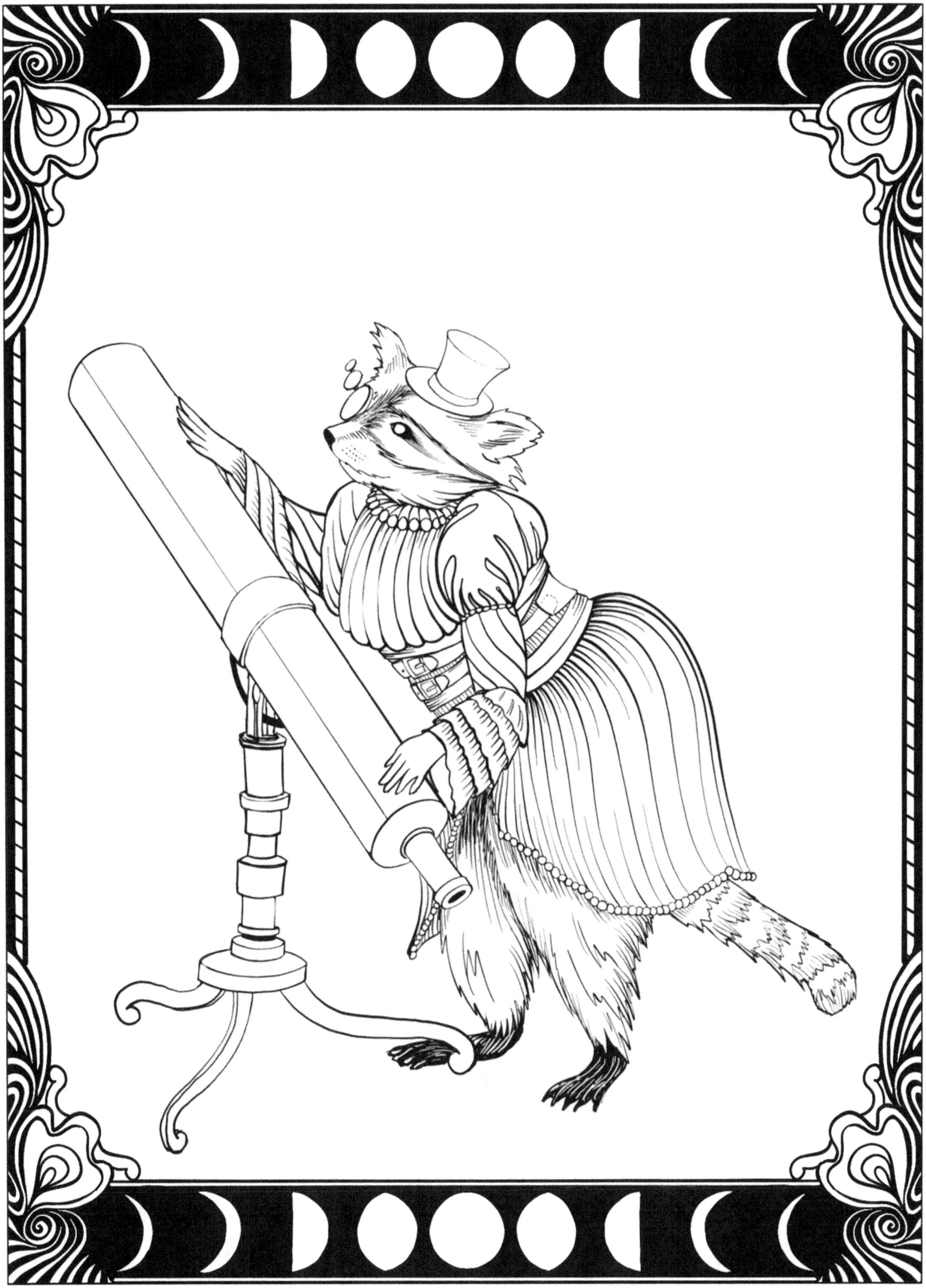

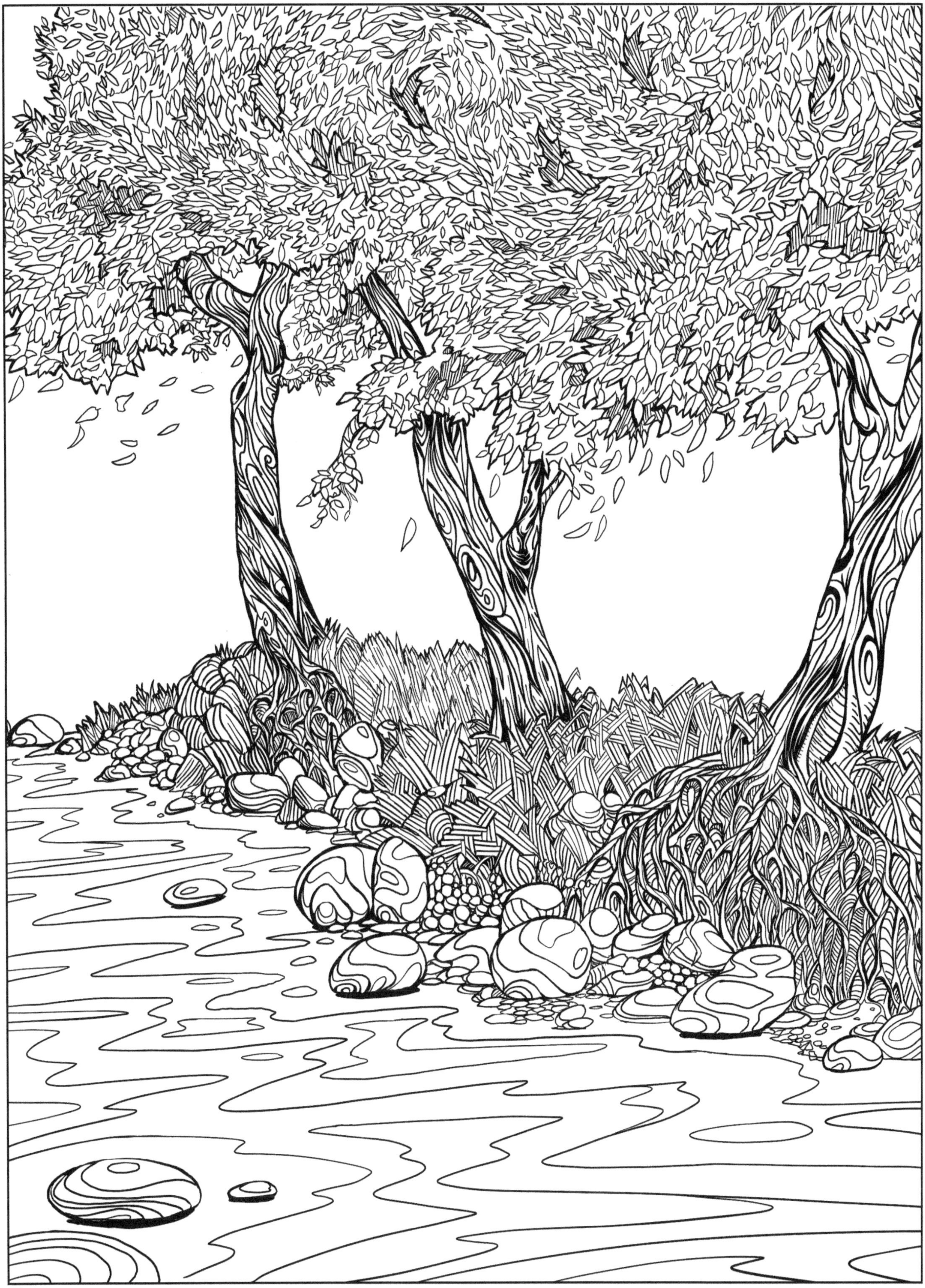

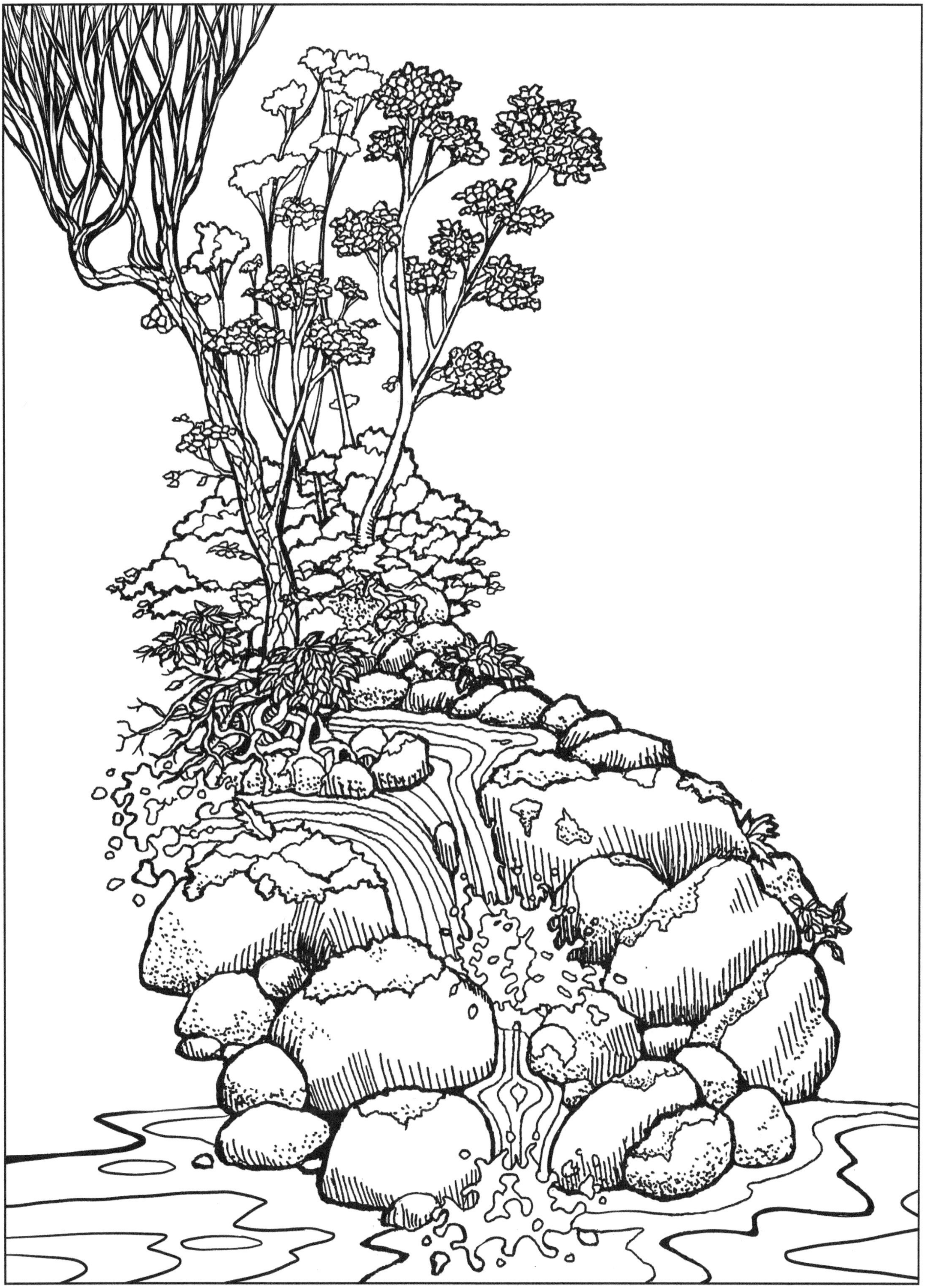

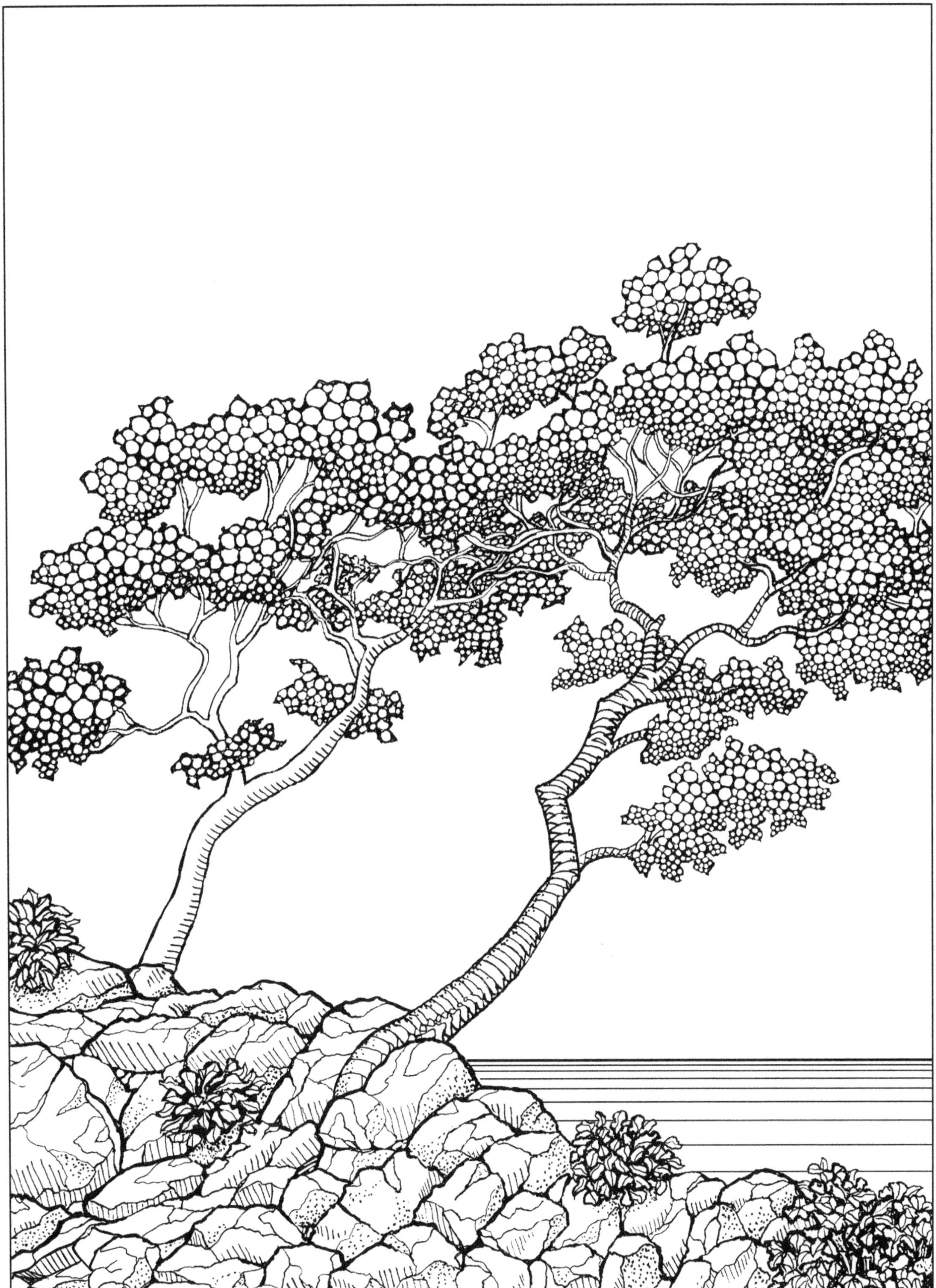

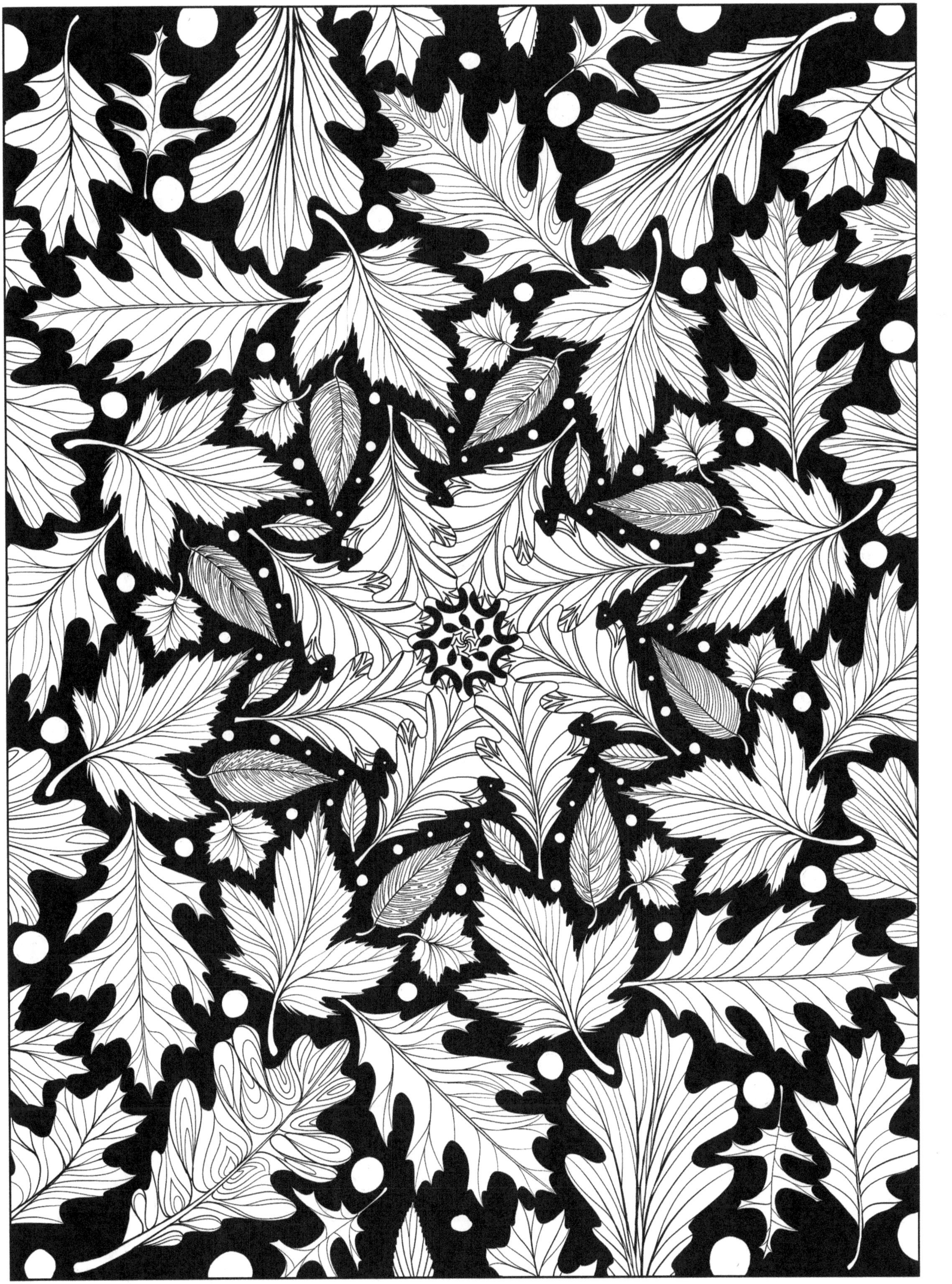

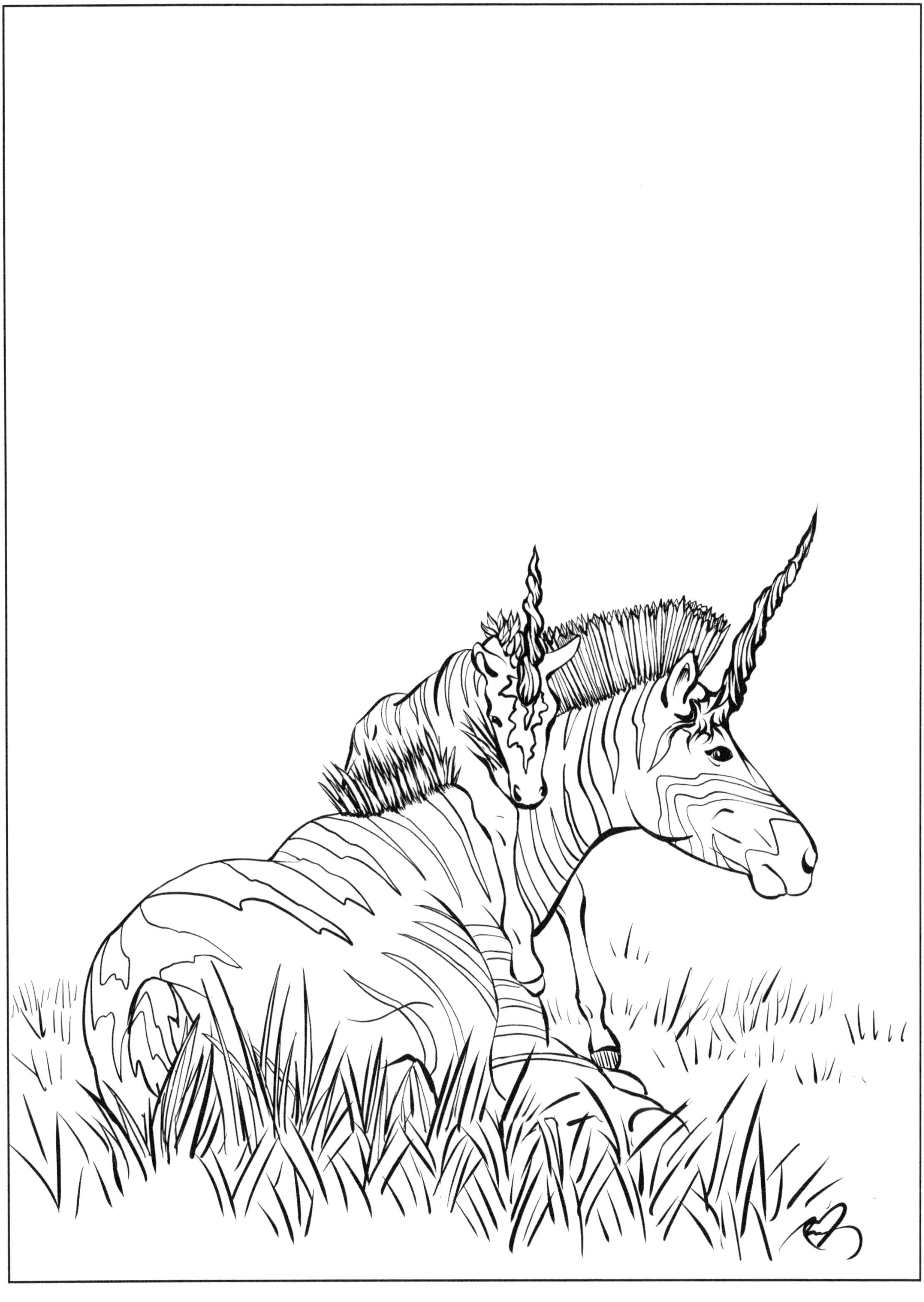

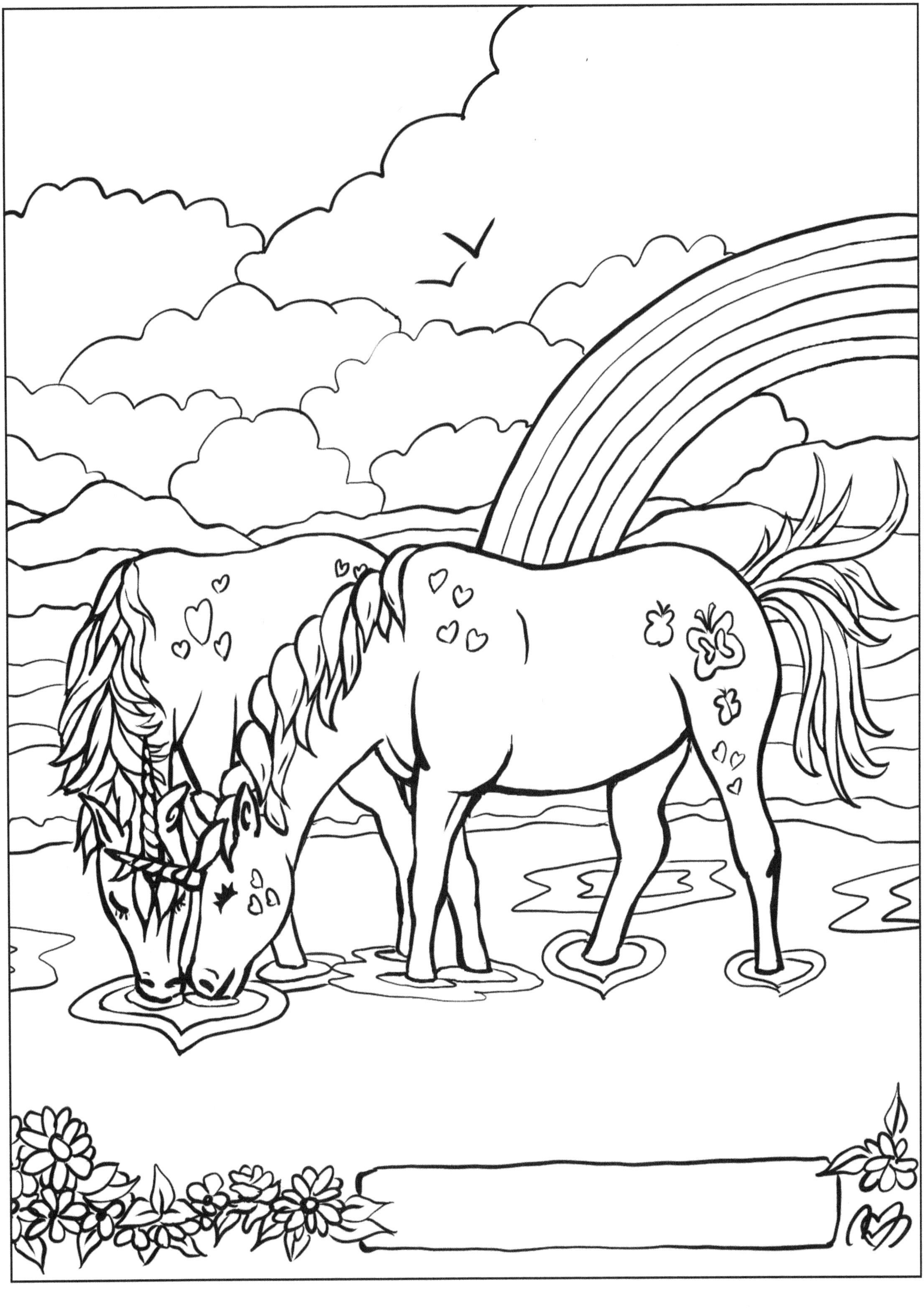

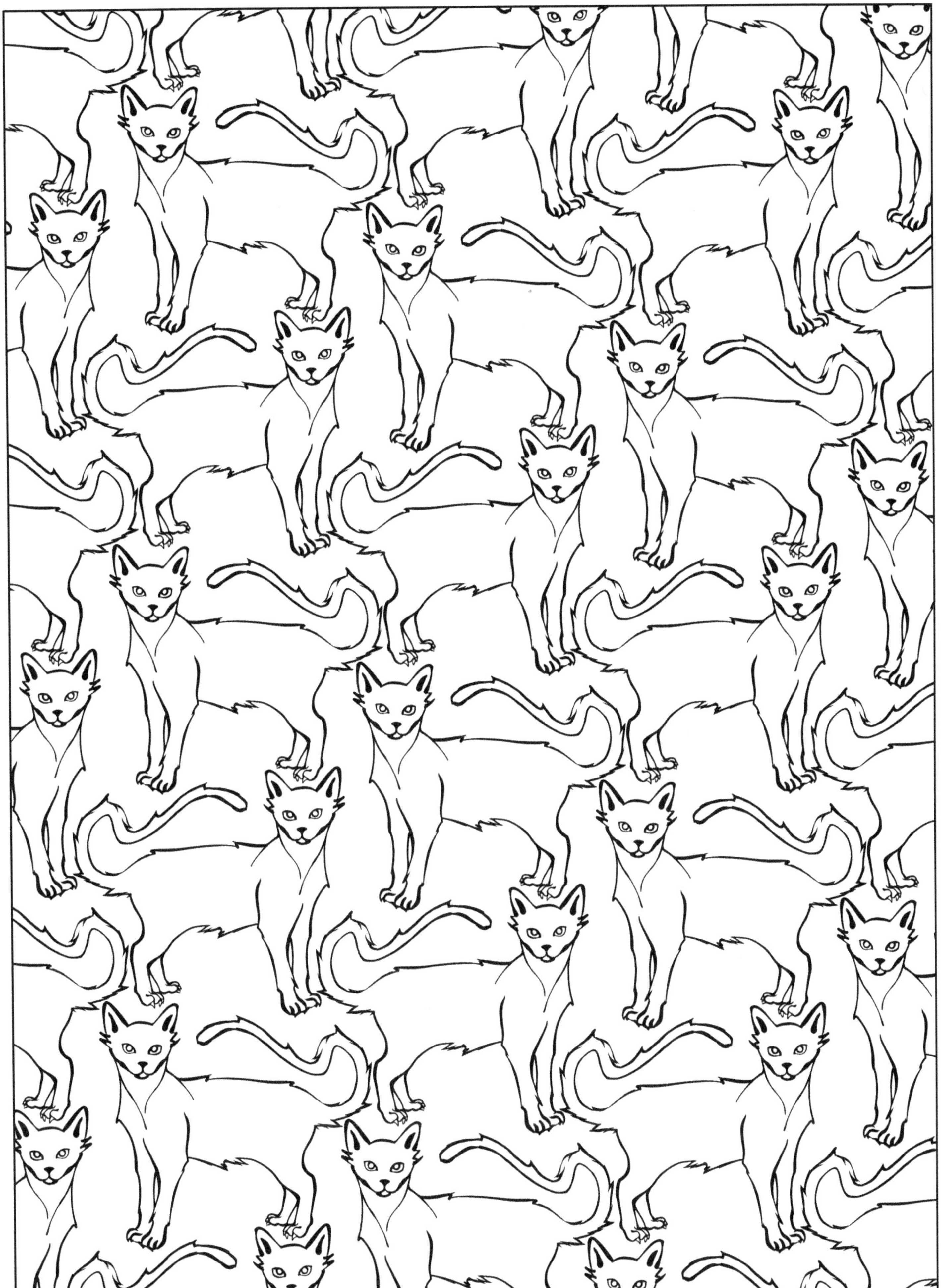

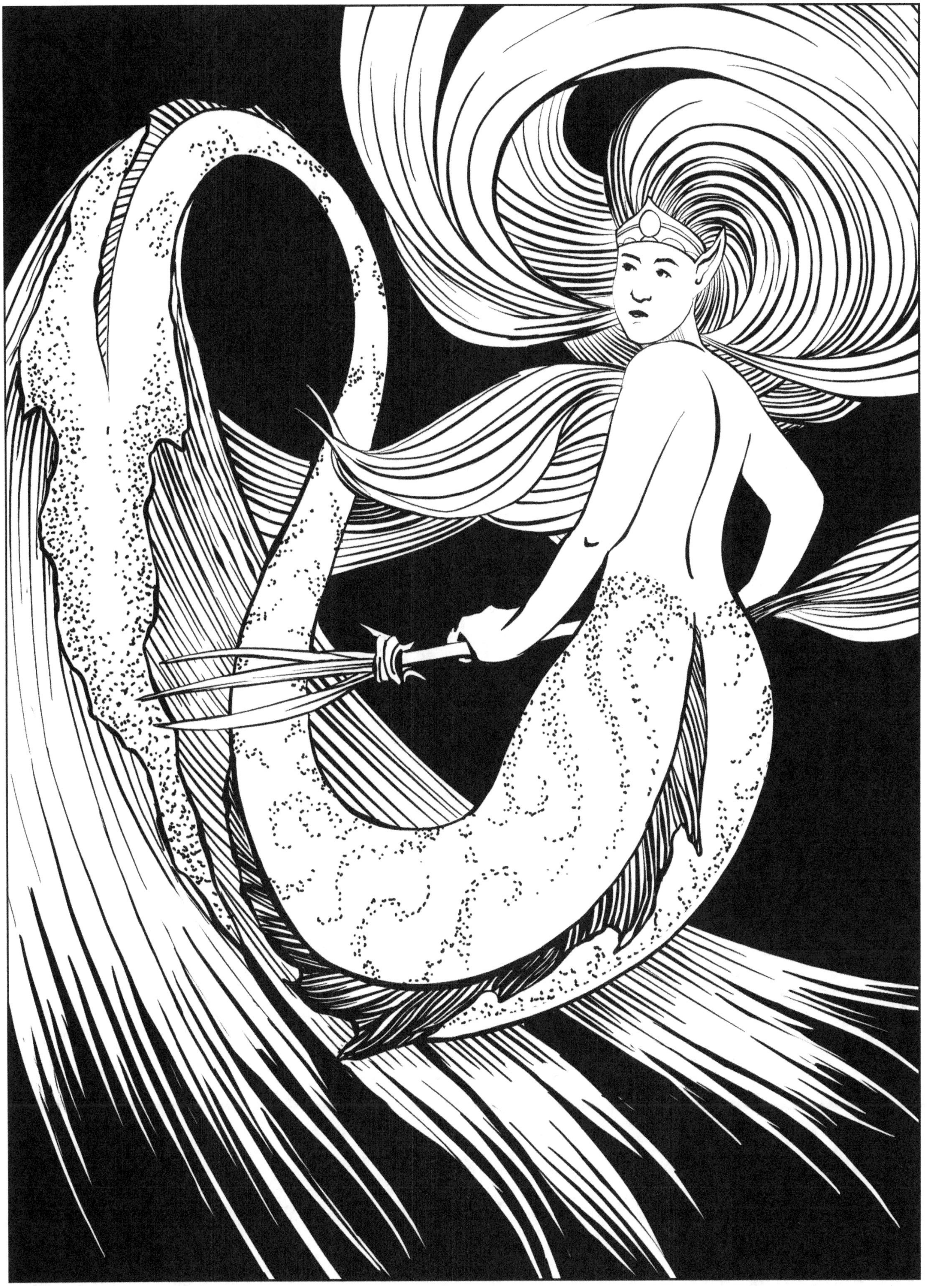

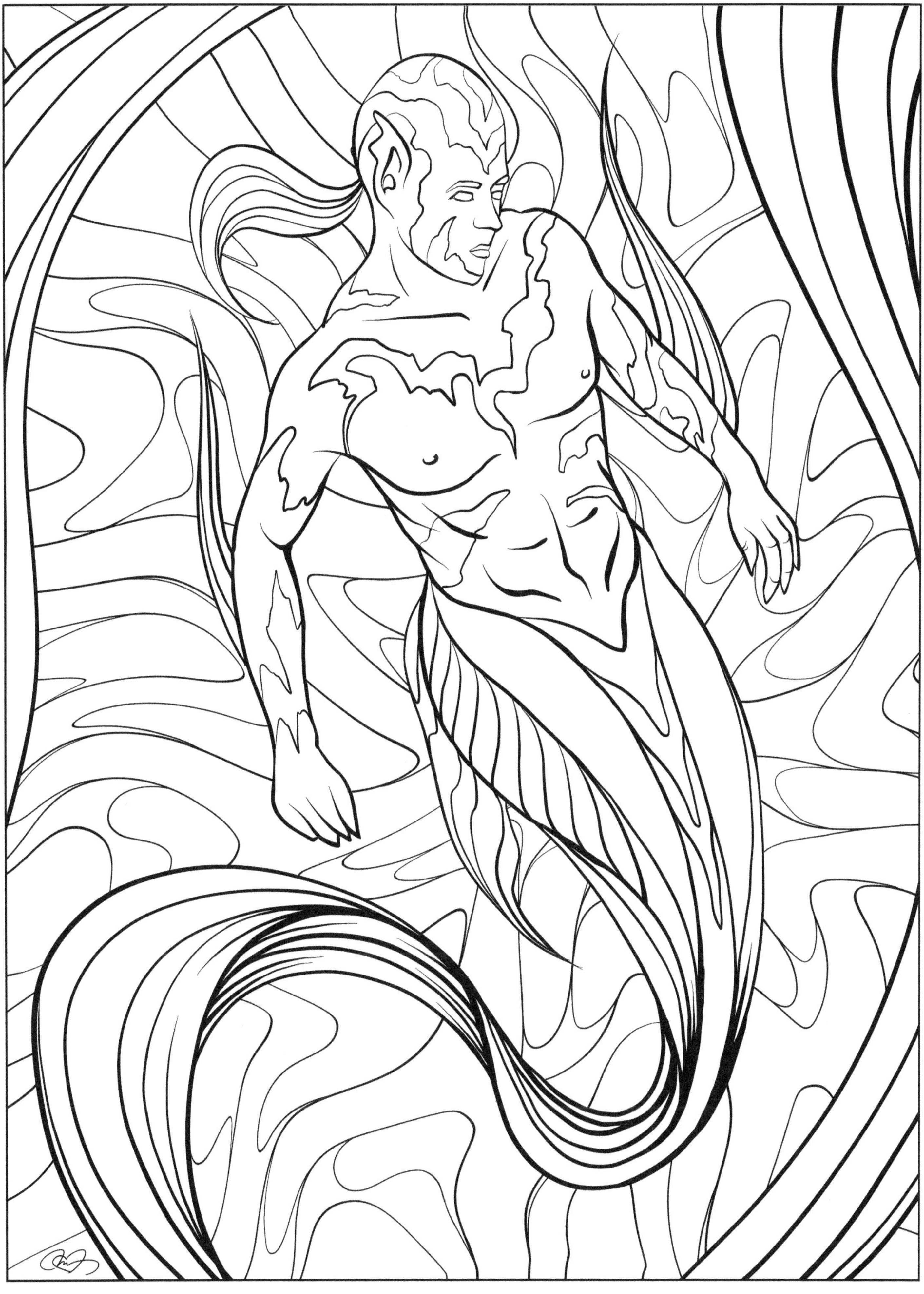

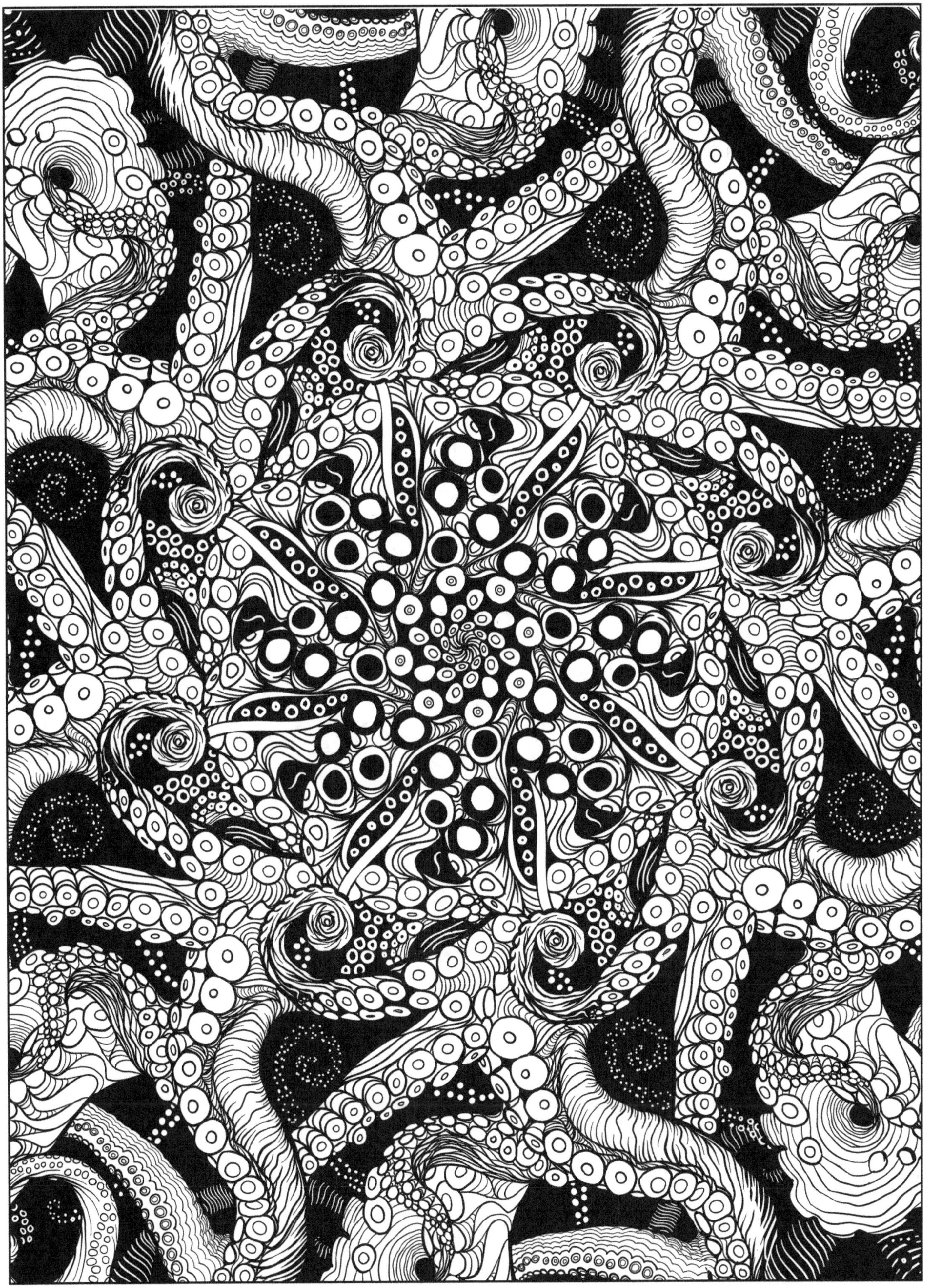

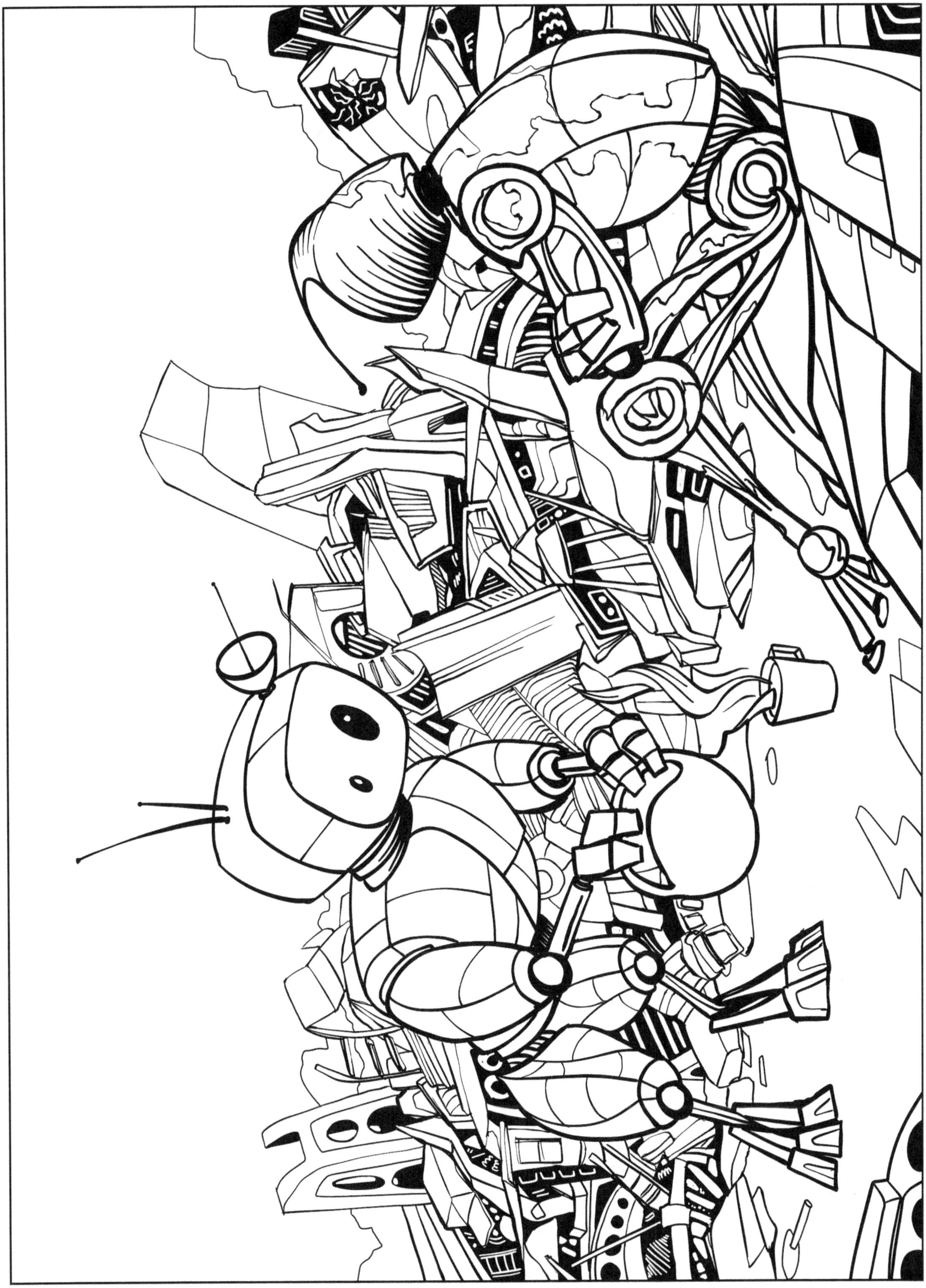

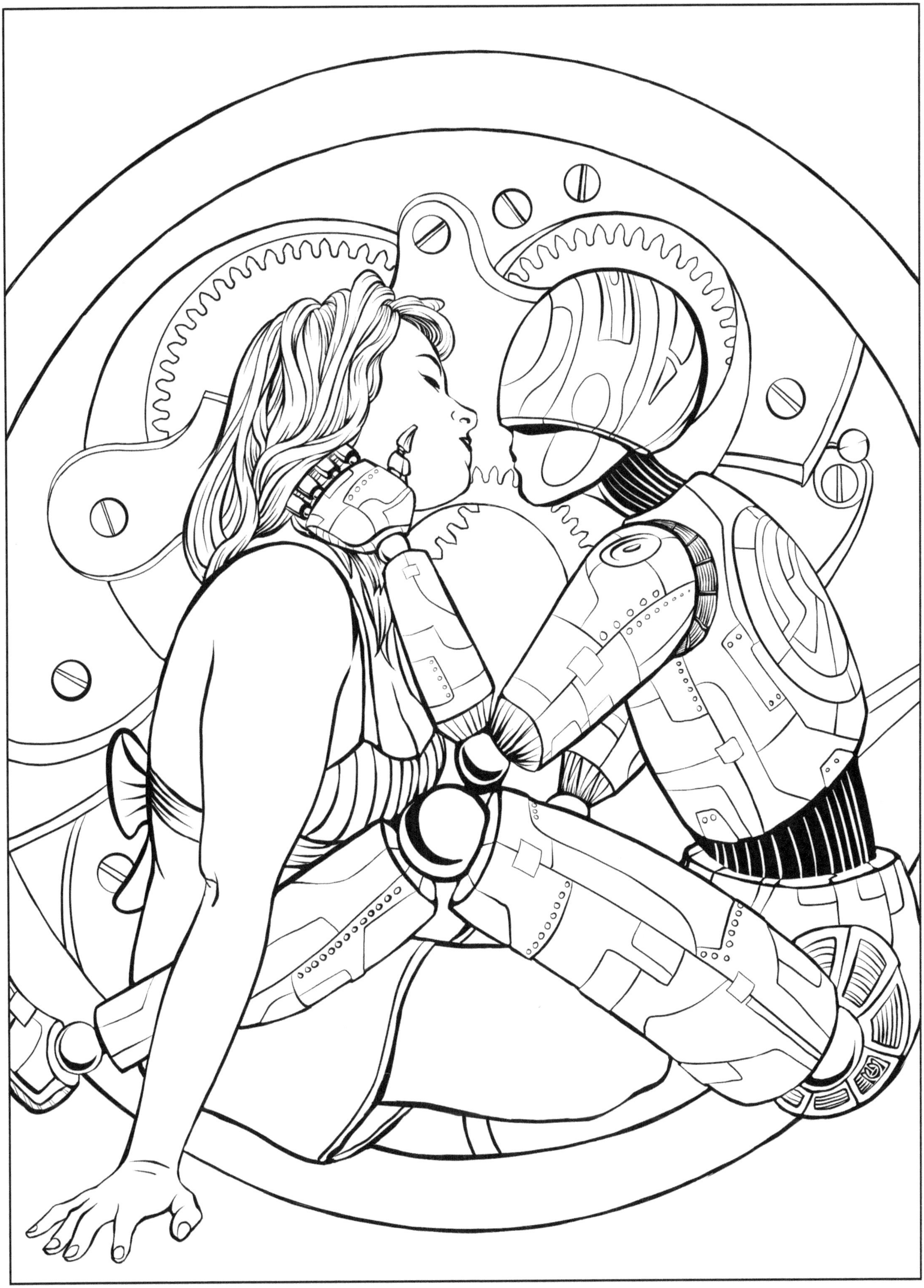

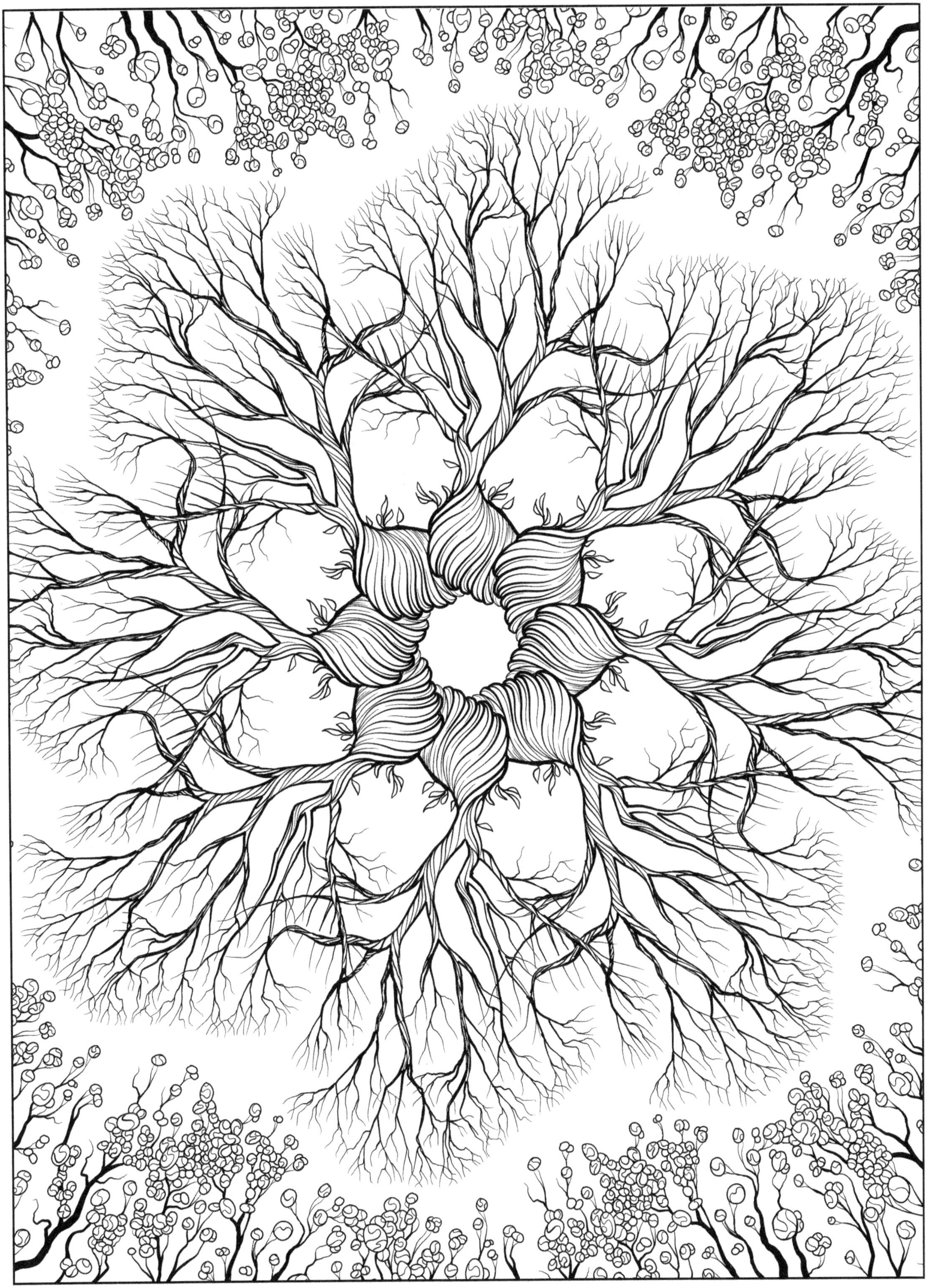

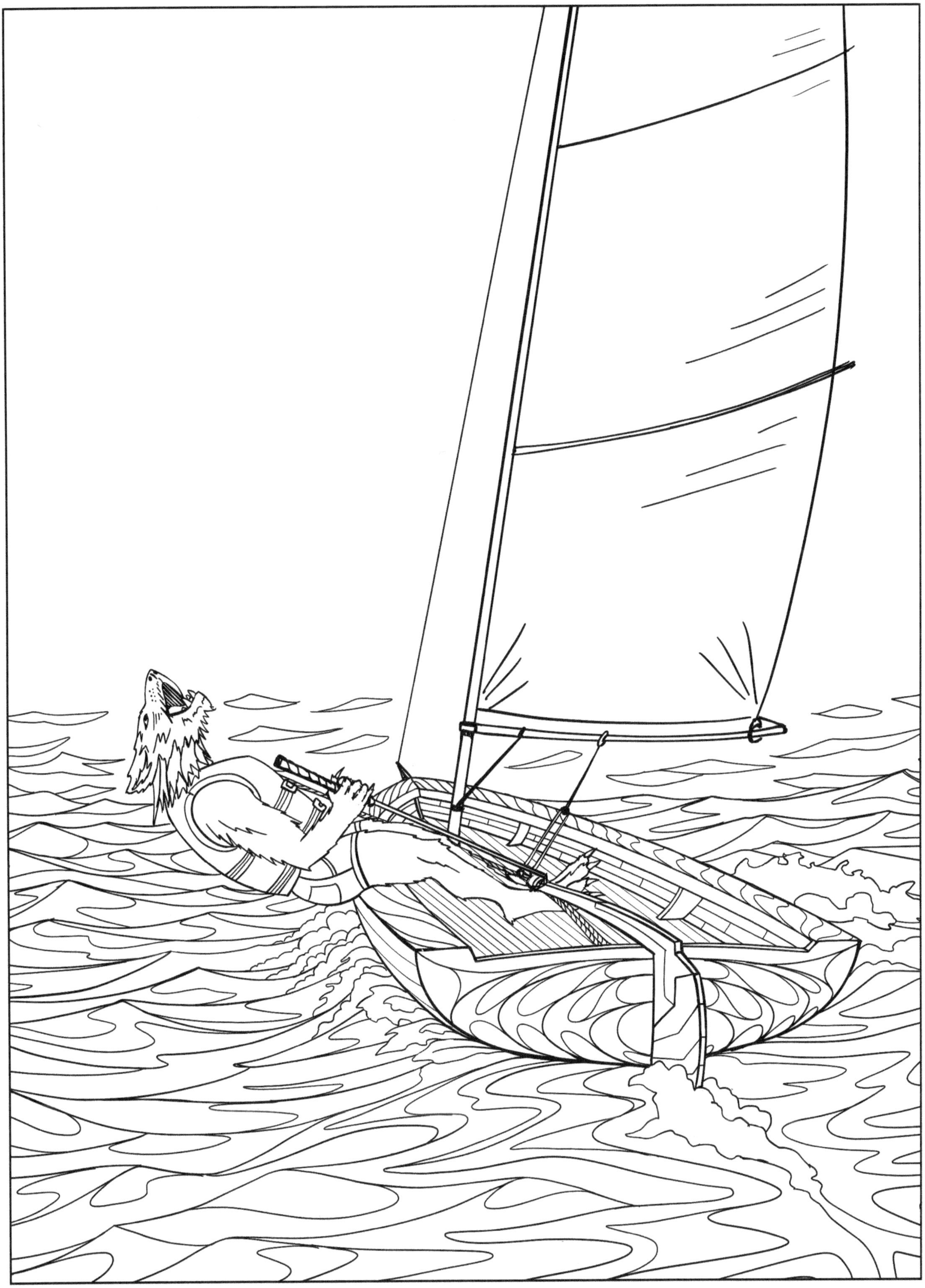

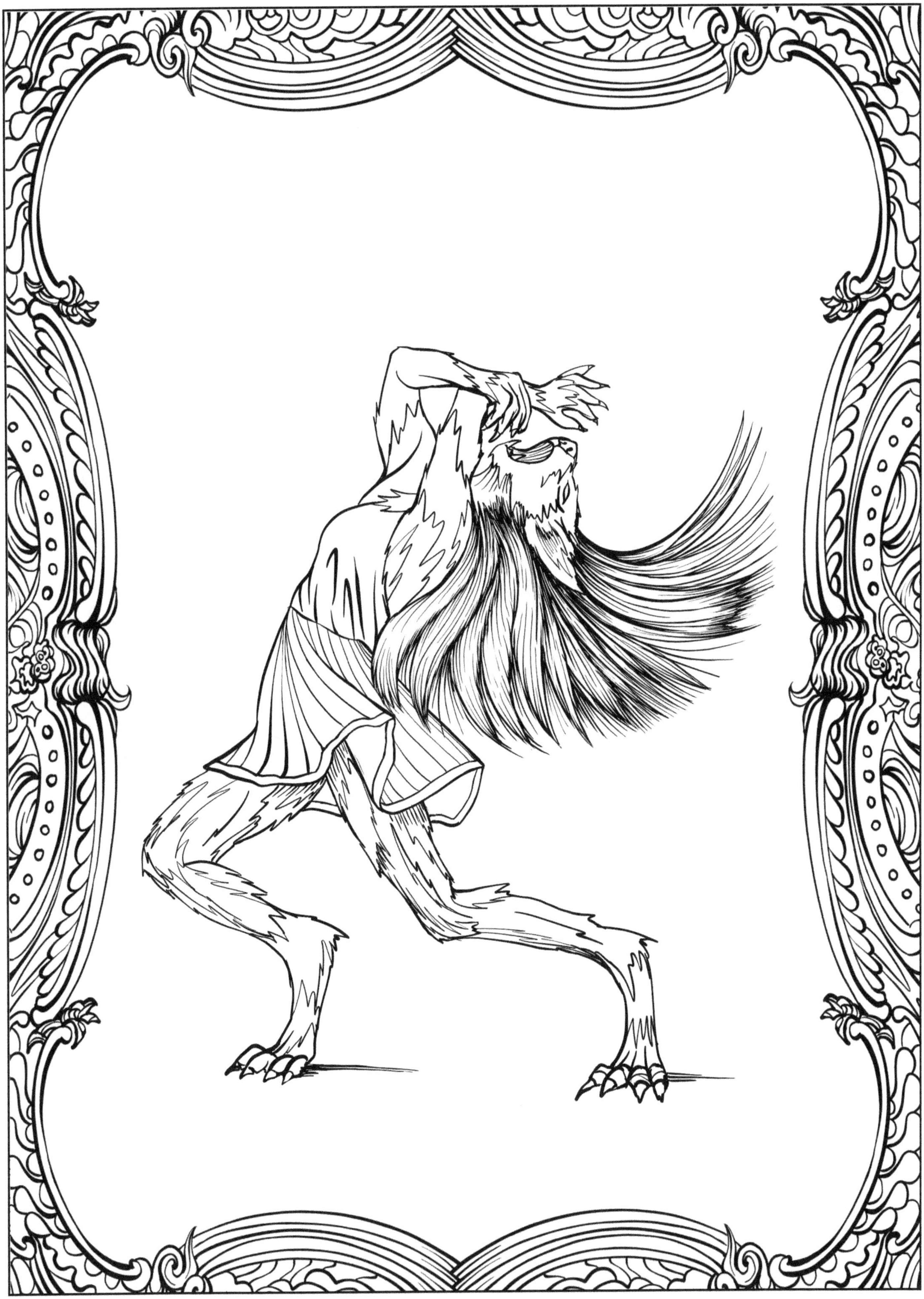

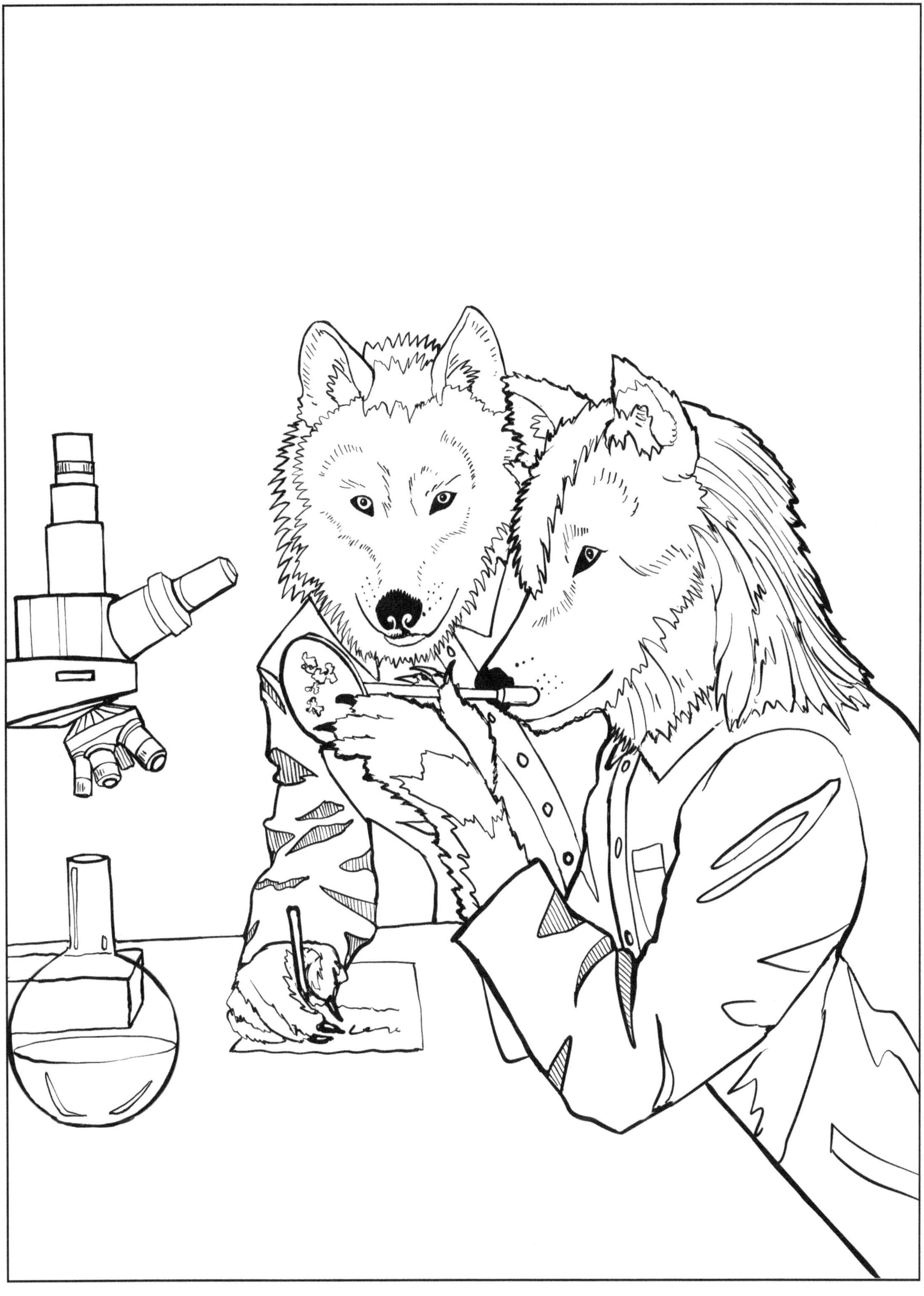

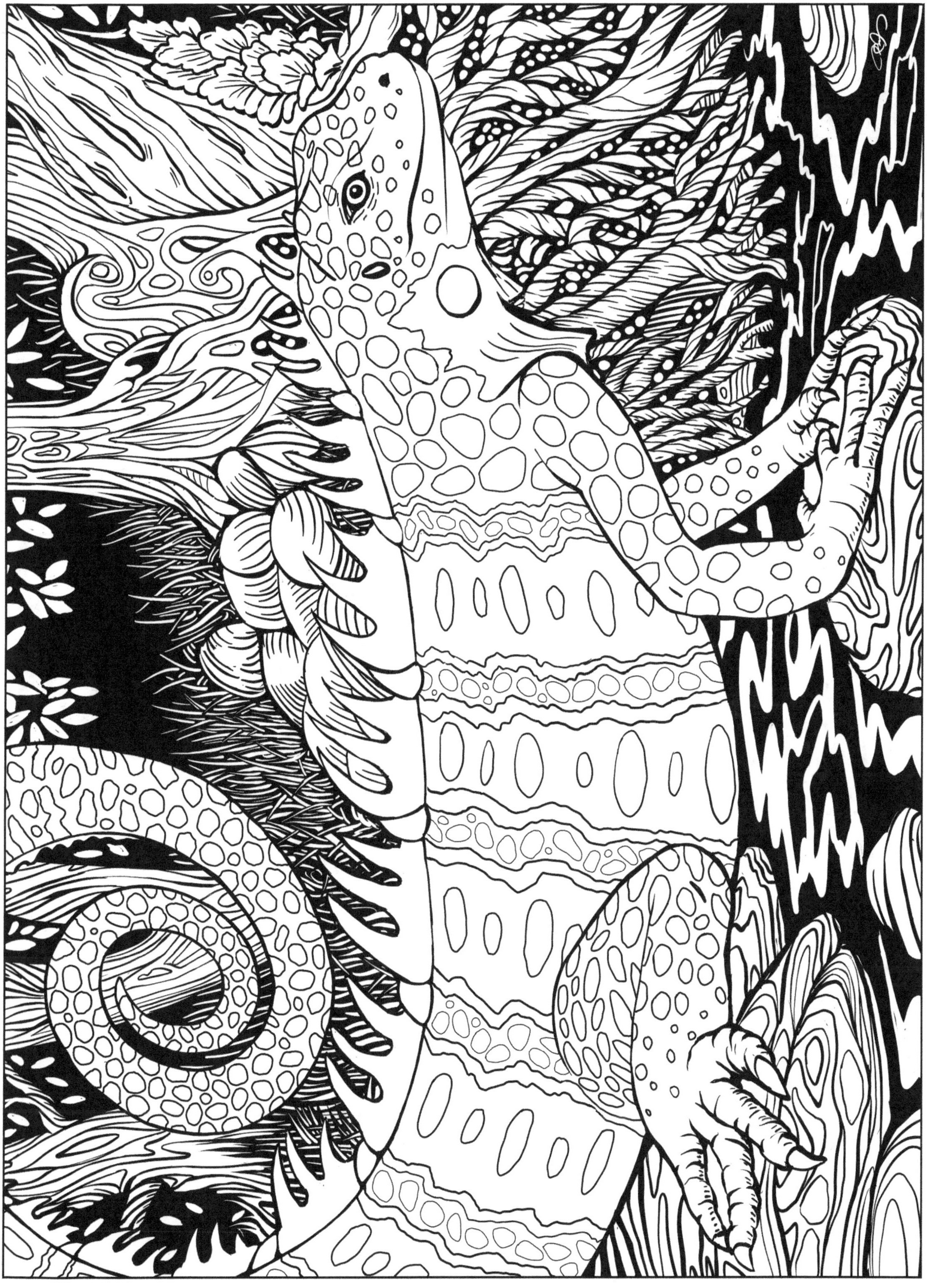

www.ingramcontent.com/pod-product-compliance
Lightning Source LLC
Chambersburg PA
CBHW062341220526
45469CB00008B/2795
* 9 7 8 1 7 2 6 8 4 0 6 0 6 *